SEASONS TO CELEBRATE

God's Children CELEBRATE the Church Year

by MARY E.F. ALBING

Augsburg Fortress, Minneapolis

CONTENTS

SEASONS TO CELEBRATE
God's Children Celebrate the Church Year

Mary E.F. Albing, writer
Barbara S. Wilson, Randi Sundet Griner, and Rich Gordon, editors
Lecy Design, cover
RKB Studios, illustrations

Scripture quotations marked NRSV are from New Revised Standard Version Bible, copyright 1989
Division of Christian Education of the National Council of the Churches of Christ in the United States
of America. Used by permission.

Manufactured in U.S.A.

2 3 4 5 6 7 8 9 0 1 2 3 4 5 6 7 8 9

INTRODUCTION

Time, Seasons, and Holiness

The Western notion of time is linear. Most modern people think in terms of days, months, and years arranged on some kind of time line that takes us back into the past and stretches ahead of us into the future. The year 1901 followed 1900, 1902 followed 1901, and so on until the present year, just as today followed yesterday and 11 o'clock followed 10 o'clock. Linear time continues to add minutes, hours, days, and years, in order.

But when we enter the seasons of the church year, we enter into an entirely different concept of time. Like the rhythms of the natural world—planting and harvest, birth, death, and rebirth—the church year moves in a circle rather than along a line. Its calendar is arranged according to celebrations of events that occurred hundreds of years ago, and it ritually repeats those celebrations each year.

Moreover, the moment we begin to worship we engage in holy time. The holy time of worship is concerned with the wholeness and well-being of participants as they relate to their God. Our ritual acts, which give that holy time its shape, help us remember important past events in our relationship with God. These acts reenact the fullness of the gospel story. But we do not simply recount what happened in the past. Time itself is different in ritual.

As we remember past events we experience them again—individually and as a community—and we look forward to experiencing them in the future. We feel the healing of the blind man, we accept the challenge to the woman at the well. On Easter morning we hear the amazed declaration, "He is risen," from the women who found the tomb empty. And we respond with the men and women of long ago, "He is risen indeed." These words remind us of the resurrection event nearly 2000 years ago. We experience the new life of resurrection today, and at the same time express our hope for the resurrection at the end of time. Ritual time always works that way. Jesus is for us—yesterday, now, and forever.

Word and Symbols

The gospel comes to us in word, the ongoing story of God's deep love for us. The word is about a savior who came washing feet, bearing brutality and bondage to death so that we need not, and rising so that we might be free and have new life. The gospel comes to us in word and in the Word, the free gift who is Jesus Christ, to whose gift we can add nothing.

When we enter the seasons of the church year, we encounter a number of symbols. We are accustomed to symbols. We live in a visual culture, filled with symbols of health and illness, success and failure, freedom and oppression. From storefronts and highways to newspapers and television, we are constantly interpreting a variety of symbols. Symbols are a way of life for us.

There is, however, an intrinsic problem with symbols. Most symbols, by their very nature, may be interpreted in more than one way. An example is the heart. It may be simply a cute decoration or the sign for a place to donate blood. A heart-shaped pillow given to one who has survived heart surgery is a reminder of life. But encased in lace and sent on Valentine's Day, it says "I love you."

From its beginning, the Christian community has used symbols to help express, explore, and explain some of the complexities and mysteries of faith. Word, water, cross, bread and wine—each enrich our understandings of God who is for us and with us. The gospel comes to us first in word and story, but it also comes through symbols. Rituals also help us encounter the good news, God news, in dramatic ways. Through rituals of liturgy, worship, and sacrament we express important and powerful feelings and needs. God's word addresses those feelings and needs—equipping us to deal with rites of passage, the rhythms of life and seasons, failure, confession, and healing, our deepest longings, fears, and joys.

There is strength and hope in a community that gathers around and affirms word, symbol, and ritual. Growing children in the faith involves teaching the story to live the good news and to encourage sacred expression.

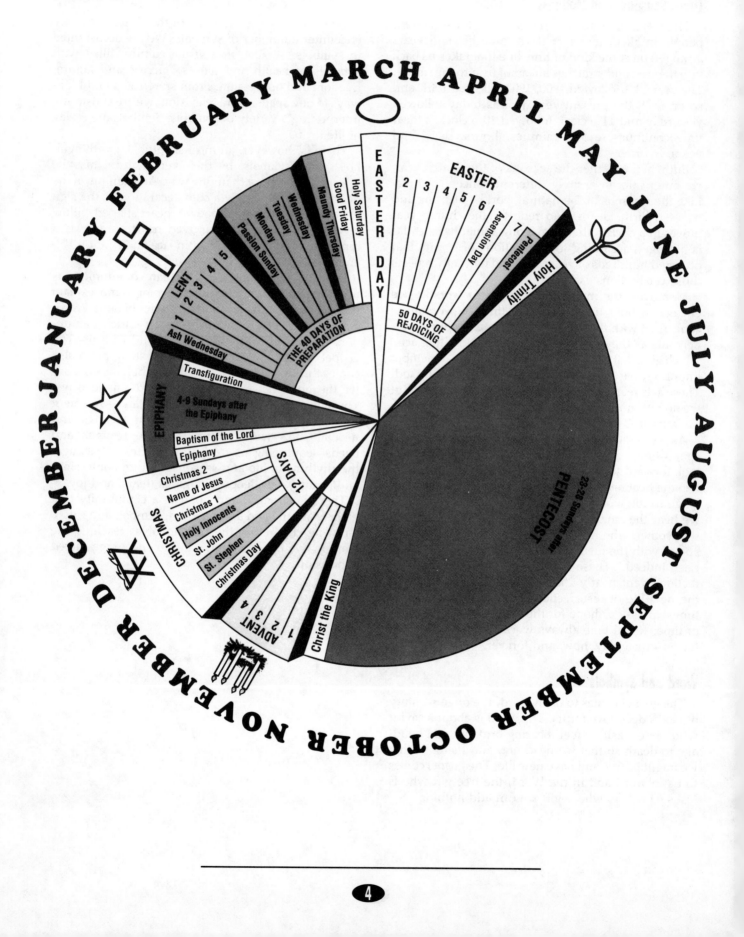

OVERVIEW

Seasons to Celebrate gives you and your church ways to learn about and celebrate the major festivals of the church year. Ideas for activities, crafts and community outreach are developed from the Bible stories and symbols associated with each season. Intergenerational events and activities for each season are included.

The Season of . . .

This begins each season's section with a description of that season of the church year, based on Bible stories and stories from a variety of cultures.

A Symbol

This provides a focus for activities and crafts. The traditional colors of the seasons are highlighted and explained.

A Sign

A key word or concept related to the season is introduced using the language of sign. Leaders may incorporate each sign into worship, music, and activities however they wish.

Songs

Songs are part of any seasonal celebration. Most churches have access to both traditional and contemporary music to meet a variety of needs. Several song suggestions are included at the beginning of each season. Choose among them and others available to you based on the ages of participants, the skill of your music leaders, and coordination with music used in your church's worship.

Activities

Here, activities and crafts are laid out in detail for every age level for each season. Intergenerational ideas are found throughout.

Celebrating . . .

This gives suggestions for worship experiences designed to help children and adults develop a sense of the sacred. Included are litanies, songs from many cultures, and a variety of celebrations tied to the season and its symbol.

Around the Table

Learning about the seasons of the church year can continue at home. Families may use the information, prayer, Bible references, and questions on pages 56-61 to wonder and explore together each of the seasons. Note the permission to make photocopies of those pages.

Send to each home a copy of the appropriate page at the beginning of the season. You might photocopy the pages on paper that is a seasonal color. Consider distributing them in Sunday school, at intergenerational events, and as inserts in bulletins and newsletters.

Show how the page may be folded lengthwise to stand on a family table.

ADVENT

THE SEASON OF HOPEFUL WAITING

As a culture, we are not very good at waiting. We feel that we can and should control much of our lives. But the yearly seasons come and go with power, on their own schedule, and insist that we wait. These seasons (echoed in the seasons of the church year) remind us that we must give up control, admit our powerlessness, and put our hope in God's grace.

Advent is the perfect time to teach children (and adults) about waiting and hope, because the time before Christmas is one of great excitement. Children look forward to gifts, special foods, parties and programs, and visits with members of their extended families. They only need to connect their great anticipation with the Christian tradition of waiting for something much greater—the gift of God's Son.

Areas far from the equator experience the seasonal changes dramatically. Ancient peoples mourned the loss of daylight as the winter deepened, just as we do today. They knew that warmth, longer days, and the outdoor activities of tending animals and planting crops would return. But they didn't understand how or why. They took the cold weather as an instruction from heaven, and they slowed down, bowing to the wind, the cold, and the darkness.

And so the church year begins with creation waiting, sleeping. Advent, dark and mysterious, pulls us into the rhythm of God's time, holy time, with the promise of light. Along with Mary, we wait—for that light, for a child to be born. Emmanuel.

The First Sunday in Advent

This is when believers are called to be watchful. We children of light look at the darkness around us and within us and remember that light will return. The time will come when even the light of the sun or moon will not be needed. The glory of God and the light of the lamb will be enough (Revelation 22:5). In Advent, as we prepare to celebrate Jesus' birth we also watch for his second coming.

The Second Sunday in Advent

We long with the psalmists for God's peace on earth, and we pray with the angels for good will to all people.

The Third Sunday in Advent

We hope with John the Baptist and the prophets for the coming of the Messiah who will be the light of the world.

The Fourth Sunday in Advent

Christmas is within view, and we are caught up in Mary's song of joy.

A SYMBOL: THE WREATH

The Advent wreath has its origins in pre-Christian northern Europe, especially Germany. Winter was the season to slow down, to stop normal activity and wait, hoping for spring. Once the snow came, each household would take a wheel from a wagon, bring it inside, and decorate it with an assortment of greens, dried flowers, and candles. There the wheel stayed until spring. With these wheels, light came in for the winter, a sign of a different time, a changing time.

Missionaries adapted this pagan custom to communicate the Christian message of hope and relate it to the birth of Christ. The wheel became a wreath, its roundness reminding us that God is eternal and its evergreens symbolizing everlasting life.

The wreath draws us into non-linear, God-time, sacred and cyclical time. It reminds us to slow down and wait. Its four candles relate to the Bible texts for the weeks before Christmas. They represent watchfulness, peace, hope, and joy as they prepare us for Jesus' birth. Week by week, as another candle is lit, the light of Christ slowly increases the light in our lives until we celebrate Christ's coming on Christmas.

The color for Advent is blue, the traditional color of hope. (Purple may be used as well because Advent is a time for reflection. For many centuries Advent was viewed as a time of penance in preparation for Christmas.) The word *Advent* means "coming." During this season, whether our hearts are light or heavy, extraneous things are set aside and we focus on preparing for Christ's coming.

A SIGN: WAIT/WAITING

SONGS FOR ADVENT

"Rejoice, Rejoice, Believers"
"Wake, Awake, for Night Is Flying"
"Oh, Come, Oh, Come, Emmanuel"
"Come, Thou Long-Expected Jesus"
"Kum Ba Yah"
"I've Got the Joy, Joy, Joy, Joy Down in My Heart"

ADVENT ACTIVITIES

Holy Time Wheel Wreath

You will need:
- wheels of many sizes
- scissors
- candles
- dried branches, weeds, and flowers
- evergreen branches
- strings of lights
- wire of various weights
- red or blue ribbon

Begin the celebration of Advent by making Advent wreaths that are real reminders to enter holy time. Individuals, families, and groups create wreaths using wheels from wagons, bicycles, toy cars, or even real tractors that will be put away for the winter. Choosing the wheel will be an important part of the activity. The size of the wheel can be determined by the age of the wreathmaker and the place where it will be displayed. For example, a preschooler could decorate a tricycle tire to hang on her or his closet door. The building and grounds committee could decorate a large wheelbarrow wheel and set it up by the church's front door. Very small wheels may be made into tree decorations.

After explaining the wheel/wreath and its significance for Advent, let participants create their wreaths. Have on hand an assortment of greens, gnarly branches, and dried flowers and weeds, as well as candles and strings of lights that they may use for decorating.

Be available with whatever suggestions and help are needed, especially with younger children. Consider singing Advent and Christmas hymns as you work. Be enthusiastic about differences among the wreaths—each will be unique.

Finish each wreath by tying a ribbon at the bottom and attaching a loop of wire or string at the top for hanging. Tie a ribbon in a bow on the bottom of the wreath.

Advent Calendar

Everyone enjoys preparing for Christmas by making an Advent calendar. Many Advent calendars are available for purchase, usually with doors that open to reveal Bible verses, tiny pictures, or even treats. Let individuals, families, or other groups of people make their own, perhaps using some recycled materials. Offer options for calendars as simple and complex, large and small as possible.

Consider providing:
- cardboard circles with 25 spaces—numbered and dividable as puzzle pieces.
- rectangular coloring book-style drawings on white paper with windows to open, and a second layer of paper below with spaces outlined to match the windows.
- lists of short, appropriate Bible verses, and of helpful things to do—at home, at church, and in the community.
- Advent symbol stickers, magazine or greeting card cutouts and glue for collages, markers and construction paper

Cranes

You will need:
- foldable paper squares, 4" and larger
- string or cord

Advent is a time to remember that God calls us to peace. The story of Sadako and the Thousand Paper Cranes connects Japanese tradition with human longing for peace, especially in the aftermath of war. Introduce the activity by telling this story:

Sadako Sasaki was a three-year-old Japanese girl who lived in Hiroshima when the atomic bomb was dropped there in 1945. Ten years later she died of "atom bomb disease," a leukemia caused by large amounts of radiation.

According to Japanese legend, cranes live for a thousand years, and anyone who folds a thousand paper cranes will be granted a wish. Before her death, Sadako folded 644 paper cranes, and with each one wished that she would recover from her illness. Her friends continued folding cranes after she died, so that she could be buried with 1000 beautiful origami cranes.

Children throughout Japan heard about Sadako, and sent money to build a memorial to her and to remind all people to work for peace. The Children's Peace Monument, a statue of Sadako holding a golden crane, is in Hiroshima Peace Park. The words on the monument are: "This is our cry, This is our prayer, Peace in the world."

Suggest that each paper crane made be a prayer for peace. Consider hanging a string of cranes around your church doorways to remind people as they leave to work for God's peace in the world.

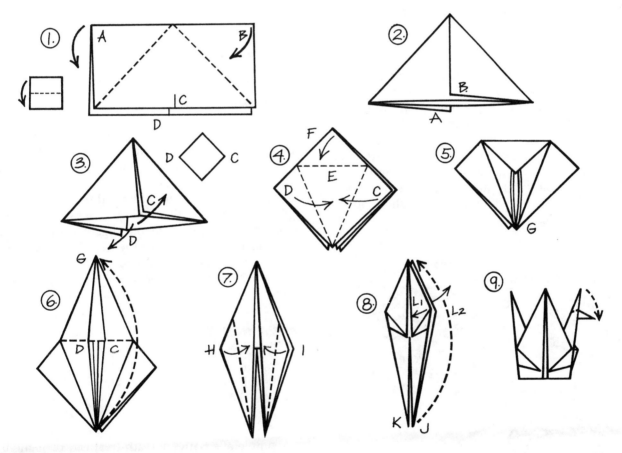

1. Fold a square piece of paper in half horizontally. Then fold A back to bottom center (*D*), and B *forward* to front bottom center (C).

2. Your paper should look like this.

3. Pull C (the front) and D (the back) apart all the way until you have a flat diamond (as in small diagram).

4. Fold top layers of C and D inward to center line at E and fold down F along dotted line.

5. Your paper should look like this.

6. Now here's the tricky part: Unfold step 4. Take top layer *only* at G and pull it up making use of the crease (dotted line). This allows points C and D to fold back to center line along creases. Turn paper over and repeat steps 4, 5 and 6, ignoring new flap topped by point G.

7. With split at bottom, fold H and I inward so that edges meet center line. Turn paper over and repeat.

8. Temporarily open flaps at L_1 and L_2. Pull J up to top between flaps and close flaps (L_1 and L_2). Repeat with K. Fold down head. Fold down wings.

Advent Journal

Older children and adults as well as families can create waiting journals. Use medium-sized blue spiral notebooks. Label the front, "WAITING: MY ADVENT JOURNAL." Date and decorate the corners or edges of each page for the season. On the bottom of each page you may wish to write a Bible verse or a prayer. Worship texts for the Sundays in Advent include:

First Sunday: Matthew 24:37-44; Mark 13:33-37; Luke 21:25-36; Isaiah 2:1-5; Isaiah 63:16b-17; Isaiah 64:1-8; and Jeremiah 33:14-16.

Second Sunday: Matthew 3:1-12; Mark 1:1-8; Luke 3:1-6; Isaiah 11:1-10; Isaiah 40:1-11; and Malachi 3:1-4.

Third Sunday: Matthew 11:2-11; John 1:6-8, 19-28; Luke 3:7-18; Isaiah 35:1-10; Isaiah 61:1-3, 10-11; and Zephaniah 3:14-18a.

Fourth Sunday: Matthew 1:18-25; Luke 1:26-38; Luke 1:39-45; Isaiah 7:10-14; 2 Samuel 7:8-11, 16; and Micah 5:2-4.

Martin Luther's *Morning Prayer* and *Evening Prayer* along with the words of many Advent and Christmas hymns would be appropriate prayer sources.

Explain that a journal is place to record thoughts, feelings, hopes, dreams, and questions. Journals can be about anything, but this is a waiting journal. On each day in Advent, individuals or families can write thoughts and prayers about or draw reminders of waiting and hoping. Preparations for the season may also be included along with favorite quotations about hope and waiting.

Wreath Cookies for Sharing

Encourage people in your faith family to take time out from their busy schedules to celebrate the season by making Advent treats to share. Ask your pastor who might appreciate the treats—people who are homebound, in homeless shelters, in crisis shelters, or in hospitals or nursing homes.

During or following the food preparation, the group might enjoy time together for singing or worship. Best of all would be to deliver the treats with music.

Wreath Cookies

1 cup sugar
1 cup butter or margarine
1 egg
½ cup milk
1 teaspoon vanilla
1 teaspoon almond extract
3½ cups flour
1 teaspoon baking powder
¼ teaspoon salt
½ teaspoon green (or blue) food coloring
colored sprinkles
cookie sheets

Do ahead of time: Mix together milk, vanilla, almond extract, egg, butter, and sugar. Add salt, baking powder, and flour. Divide dough in half. Color one half with green (or blue) food coloring. Cover and refrigerate the dough for at least three hours.

To make the wreaths: Roll out a teaspoon of each color into a 4" strip on a smooth sugared surface. Twist them together gently. Shape them into a wreath, tucking the ends together. Add colored sprinkles. Bake on an ungreased cookie sheet at 375 degrees for about 10 minutes. Makes about 4 dozen cookies.

Crunchy Wreaths

1 cup chocolate chips
1 cup butterscotch chips
3 tbsp. butter or margarine
4 cups chow mein noodles
½ cup nuts

A simple alternative wreath treat can be made by melting chocolate chips and butterscotch chips with butter, and adding chow mein noodles and nuts to make a moldable mixture. Shape the slightly cooled mixture into 2" gnarly wreaths.

CELEBRATING ADVENT

Here is a four-week celebration that may be used for Sunday school openings or other group worship during Advent. Each week place a large manger and a basket of straw or shredded paper in the front of the room. Drape a blue cloth over it. Borrow or purchase a crèche. The crèche does not have to be as large as the manger. Set Mary and Joseph, the shepherds, Magi, and animals in prominent places at the back or sides of the room, far from the manger. Each week they should be moved closer. Place an Advent wreath (if possible, one that is like a wheel), with candles, beside the manger. Have matches available.

First Week in Advent

Preparation: Ask a guest dressed as the biblical master or mistress of a house (in bathrobe and sandals, with staff and money bag) to remind the group about waiting using the dialog below. If possible, have simple, light percussion instruments (such as xylophones, bells, finger cymbals, and small drums) playing gentle rhythmic patterns with the music.

Leader: Today is the first week in the season of Advent. What important day comes on December 25? Whose birthday will it be? How will you get ready? *(Encourage answers from the children especially. Be prepared with some hints about getting ready for Jesus' birth.)*

Advent is the season when we slow down a little and wait for Jesus to be born. As we wait, we will light a candle each week of Advent. Can you guess how many weeks we will wait? *(Point at each of the four candles. Ask an older child to light one candle.)*

Leader: This wreath is a wheel that has slowed down and is waiting for Jesus to come too. Let us pray and ask God's blessing on it.

Prayer: O God, whose word makes all things holy, bless this wreath. May it remind us to slow down and wait for Jesus, your Son and our Lord.
All: Amen.

Scripture: Mark 13:32-37. The guest dressed as the biblical master or mistress of the house enters and presents the following paraphrase of the text:

Guest: Keep waiting! Be alert! So that you can be ready when Jesus comes! It is the same as when I go on long journeys. I have people who keep my household for me. Yes, I do. And they have to keep everything in good shape. *(Rub hands together.)* All those dishes have to be done. Everything must be dusted and swept properly. *(Run a finger along a table, chair, or piano.)* When I get home, I expect everything to be just right. *(Make an OK sign with thumb and middle finger.)* Otherwise, they are in big trouble! And what I say to them, I say to you: Keep waiting! Be alert! So that you can be ready when Jesus comes!

Leader: Each week of Advent, we will prepare for Jesus by adding straw (or shredded paper) to the manger. Remember things that you do for others and that you see others do to prepare for Jesus' coming, and each week we will add some soft bedding for each caring, waiting act. *(Invite several children and adults to name things and then come forward and to add straw or paper.)* Remember, Advent is the season of watching and waiting for Jesus to come. We pray for him to come in a song.

Song: "Oh, Come, Oh, Come, Emmanuel"

Second Week in Advent

Leader: Today we will once again prepare for Jesus by adding to his manger. *(Explain that people who remember caring, preparing things that they have done or seen done in the past week can add straw or paper to the manger.)*

Song: "Kum Ba Yah"

Leader: It is the second Sunday of Advent. Today we can light two candles on our Advent wreath. The wreath is a wheel, a circle that reminds us of God's forever love. It also reminds us to slow down and watch and wait for Jesus. *(Ask an older child to light the first and second candles.)* We just sang a prayer for Jesus to come to us with the words "Kum Ba Yah." When we light our second candle, we remember that Jesus comes with peace for us and all people. Let's continue the prayer together. As I finish each line of the prayer, I will raise my hands to signal you to say, "Jesus is coming soon."

Leader: Great, loving God, help us remember *(Raise hands)*. When we are sad and nothing goes right, still help us remember *(Raise hands)*. We know that many people are hurting people who need to hear the good news that *(Raise hands)*. When we can't wait a minute longer, remind us again *(Raise hands)*. Let all people everywhere praise you, God, for *(Raise hands)*.
All: Amen.

Leader: Long before Jesus came, people watched and waited for someone God promised to send, a savior, a Messiah, who would bring them peace. Everyone would worship God, and everyone would get along. Even the animals would get along. The wolves would lie down with lambs, leopards with goats, and lions with calves. And none of them would be hurt.

Scripture: Psalm 85:8. Say each line of this rap version of the text and have the group echo it. The strong beat falls on the capitalized words and syllables. After the last word in each line, clap twice.

Let me HEAR what the LORD God SPEAKS. *(clap clap)*
The LORD is SPEAKing PEACE. *(clap clap)*
To ALL who LOVE the LORD *(clap clap)*
The LORD is SPEAKing PEACE. *(clap clap)*

Leader: We already know this Messiah that people longed for. Can you guess who he is? He is called . . . Jesus.

Song: "Come, Thou Long-Expected Jesus" *(People of all ages will enjoy accompanying the group with simple rhythms and simple instruments as suggested above. Consider adding wood blocks to rub or hit together.)*

Third Week in Advent

Song: "Come, Thou Long-Expected Jesus"

Leader: Gather with me around the Advent wreath. Still we are waiting, but the time is coming closer. Preparations need to be made. And we have another Bible story to tell. (*An older child lights the first, second, and third candles.*)

Scripture: Based on Luke 3:7-16. Divide people into three groups. One group will be the people, one group will be the tax collectors, and one group will be the soldiers. Have a volunteer read the part of John the Baptist with a loud voice. Then tell the following story, or put it in your own words.

Leader: For many, many years the prophets had told the people that someone special was coming. They told the people to stay awake, to be watchful, because they did not know when this special person, this Messiah, might come. They told them that the Messiah would be a great leader, that he would give them peace.

Now Jesus had a cousin named John, who knew that the Messiah, Jesus, was about to come. So John preached out in the countryside and baptized people. He told the people that they were not doing the things God would want them to do. John told the people that God was sending the Messiah to them. John gave them hope.

Those who listened to John always asked him the same question.

Tax collectors: What should we do? We are tax collectors.
John: Do not cheat people.
Soldiers: What should we do? We are soldiers.
John: Do not threaten people or scare them.
People: What should we do? We are ordinary people.
John: Share your food and clothing with everyone.
All: Are you the special person God is sending, the Messiah?
John: No. I baptize you with water, but the Messiah will baptize you with the Holy Spirit. Jesus is coming soon—watch and hope.

Prayer: Jesus, as you come again to us with peace, help us see and comfort the hurt of our neighbors with your love, peace, and hope. Amen.

Leader: Today we will once again prepare for Jesus by adding to his manger. People long ago asked, "What should we do?" We can ask the same question. Jesus will tell us to care for one another. What caring things did you see or do this week to prepare for Jesus' coming? (*Invite individuals and groups to mention the things they observed and then add to the manger bedding.*)

If you have draped the manger in blue, explain that blue is the color of hope. Remind everyone to look for blue in the sanctuary during Advent, on the altar or pulpit. Tell them John and all the prophets before him were hoping for a Messiah.

Song: "Oh, Come, Oh, Come, Emmanuel"

Fourth Week in Advent

Preparation: Ask a musician in your congregation to chant the Magnificat printed below. Consider having a liturgical dance person do the coordinated actions, slowly in a dignified manner. If you are unable to find someone to chant, ask someone to read it.

Song: "I've Got the Joy, Joy, Joy, Joy Down in My Heart"

Leader: This is the fourth week of Advent, and Christmas is almost here. Today we hear about Mary's song of joy. The fourth candle on our Advent wreath is a candle of joy. We light it with the candles of watchfulness, peace, and hope to remind us how happy we are that Jesus is our Lord. Let's light all four candles, and pray a responsive prayer together. When I raise my hands, say, "We are happy that you are Lord."

Leader: *(Have a child light the first candle.)* You give us patience so that we can be watchful. *(Raise hands).*

Leader: *(Have another child light the second candle.)* You give us peace. *(Raise hands).*

Leader: *(Ask a third child to light the third candle.)* You give us your promises of light and hope. *(Raise hands).*

Leader: *(Ask a fourth child to light the fourth candle.)* You give us joy. *(Raise hands).*

All: Amen.

Scripture: Based on Luke 1:46-55 (Encourage the group to mirror the movements of the chanter or dancer. The text, a paraphrase of Mary's song of joy, is divided into 12 sections.)

1. My soul proclaims God's greatness; my spirit rejoices in God who loves me. *(Look up with arms raised, then with fists clenched, hold them to your chest.)*

2. God has chosen an ordinary person like me. *(Turn slowly around.)*

3. From now on, everyone will call me blessed by God. *(Hold hands out in various places; high, low, and to the side.)*

4. Holy God has done wonderful things for me. *(Hold up one hand with palm open and, looking up, slowly lower it.)*

5. God cares for all people who honor God. *(Bow as in prayer.)*

6. God, who is strong, takes away people's pride. *(Make a fist and bend your arm, then relax it and let your fingers go one at a time.)*

7. Our God raises up the lowly and weak, and throws down the powerful. *(Throw your arm down, as though throwing a ball, then lift it slowly up with palm reached out flat.)*

8. God gives food to the hungry, but not to the rich. *(Cross arms on chest, then throw them outward.)*

9. God's people receive God's help, according to God's promises, *(Turn to the left and stretch your left arm down and raise it slowly with elbow straight.)*

10. promises to Sarah and Abraham, and their children forever. *(Do the same to your right.)*

11. Glory to the Father, and to the Son, and to the Holy Spirit; *(Hold left hand high and strike it with the other, then shaking it as you would a tambourine.)*

12. As it was in the beginning, is now, and will be forever. Amen. *(Look up and, with fingers together, stretch your right arm across your body and move it up and around, like a rainbow.)*

Leader: Jesus is coming soon. We have prepared for him with joy. His soft bed is nearly ready. *(Allow time for final additions of straw or shredded paper to the manger, as suggested above.)*

Song: "Oh, Come, Oh, Come, Emmanuel"

CHRISTMAS

THE SEASON OF GOD WITH US

Three Stories

1. A tired young couple arrives in a dusty town just as the sun sets. It has been a long and difficult journey on foot, complicated by the fact that the young woman, barely old enough to be married, is in labor. Now out of energy and out of time, they are traveling on faith alone.

Since they have no close relatives living here, they are forced to try to find a place to stay for the night. But it is late and the town is filled with visitors. There is a census being taken—just one more aspect of the humiliating oppression of the Roman government.

And so they walk from one inn to the next, begging for a room. They will take anything, they say. Finally an innkeeper has pity on them and lets them sleep in a room with his animals. Soon the baby is born. As the animals sleepily look on, he is wrapped in what the couple can find, and the King of kings and Lord of lords is laid in a manger on a soft bed of straw. A manger has become a throne.

2. A tired young couple arrives at an airport in a foreign land. They have with them three small children, two cardboard boxes, and the name of a stranger, who is administrator of a local social service agency. They have been persecuted and harrassed for three years. They have watched family members suffer and die before their eyes. Their home was burned by their enemies two years ago, and they were forced to move to a refugee camp. There they slept on mats and quilts and ate mostly rice until they were approved for immigration to the United States.

Traveling on faith alone, they have left their homeland and the family members and friends who are still alive. Now they seek the goodwill of a new family, a congregation that will help them begin anew. They look around and notice that a man and woman hold a sign with their name printed on it. They are smiling. A smile has become a beacon of light and hope.

3. The weather has taken a turn for the worse. The highway, clear just minutes ago, has a slick coat of ice, and the night air has become a thick, white soup. Travelers are on their way home. It is Christmas Eve. But now the state patrol is closing the highway, and everyone is forced to pull off the road and seek shelter.

A farmhouse stands just off the freeway, and travelers see it as they drive slowly by. Several pull in, thinking they might be able to stay for a little while and then continue their journeys home. Hours later, the weather has not improved. But the members of the farm family, who have just received 15 unexpected guests, share their food, make plenty of coffee, read the story of Jesus' birth from Luke and sing carols with their new friends. The ordinary hospitality transforms the evening into an extraordinary blessing from God.

That is the gift of Christmas. Emmanuel, "God is with us," incarnate in Jesus, has come to earth, the new creation is begun, and nothing material will ever be the same.

A SYMBOL: THE MANGER

The manger symbolizes the ordinary becoming extraordinary, an ironic twist as God becomes flesh. Because of the incarnation, a barn becomes a palace. A poor, young couple is encircled in light. Shepherds become courtly worshipers and Magi bring gifts fit for a king in a manger. Even the lowly animals offer their beds and food, and sing the Lord Jesus to sleep. All earthly things take on new meaning when God comes to be a part of the earth.

Two thousand years later we still may notice the lowly "mangers" that hold Jesus—songs and prayers, families and friends, and those who need our love. This joyful Christmas season is only the beginning of Jesus' long journey of unconditional love. God's love reigns. Let the earth be glad!

The traditional color for Christmas is white, the color used to celebrate the major events in the life of Christ. It is the color of light and joy.

A SIGN: BABY

SONGS FOR CHRISTMAS

"What Child Is This"
"O Little Town of Bethlehem"
"Silent Night"
"Away in a Manger"
"Hark! The Herald Angels Sing"
"Go Tell It on the Mountain"
"Joy to the World"

CHRISTMAS ACTIVITIES

Finger Puppet Crèche

You will need:
- scissors
- glue
- glue gun
- felt (tan, brown, blue, purple, red, white, black, yellow)
- fabric paints (red, black, brown, silver, gold) yarn (black, brown)

Finger puppets can be made as simple or complex as you please, in sizes that fit large and small fingers. Younger children will enjoy playing with them. Older children, youth, and adults can be challenged to make them as gifts for younger children, to use them to put on a play, or to donate to children at a local crisis shelter.

Cut felt shapes with matching fronts and backs in several sizes. Have felt pieces puppetmakers may cut themselves.

Provide basic instruction for cutting, gluing, and decorating the felt to make the puppets. Encourage variety in the puppet designs, but be available to offer assistance and ideas as needed.

A set of figures should include Mary, Joseph, Jesus, and at least one Magi, one angel, and one shepherd. Particularly creative puppetmakers may also try making sheep and other stable animals, as well as a stable background.

Paper Love Chains

You will need:
- scissors
- glue
- pens
- construction paper, 2" x 8" strips

This activity may be used for a class, the church school, or as an intergenerational activity for the entire congregation. In it, we remember the love God has shown in Christ and pass that love along to others.

Each person, family, or group thinks of an act of love to carry out during the Christmas season, and writes or draws a reminder of it on two strips of paper. One strip becomes part of the congregational love chain. The pieces are glued together into a long chain of love and hung in a prominent place in the classroom or hallway. The other goes home, where it may be hung on a tree or wreath.

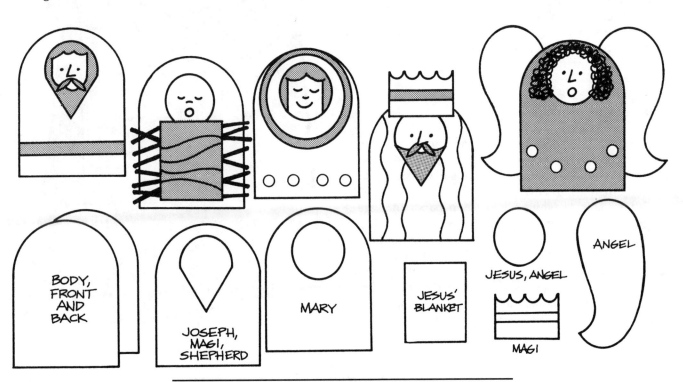

Clay Ornaments

God came to earth as a little baby. God still comes to us in the lowly "mangers" around us. With the most ordinary ingredients, we can praise God and celebrate Jesus' extraordinary birth.

You will need:
- clay
- cookie cutters in Christmas shapes (stars, trees, wreaths)
- rolling pin
- table knives
- spatula
- glitter
- nail

Basic recipe for clay:
4 cups all-purpose flour
1 cup salt
1½ cups water

Mix ingredients and knead about five minutes. Roll dough out no more than ¼" thick. Cut shapes with cookie cutters. Use a nail to poke a hole for string before baking. Bake at 350 degrees for 1 hour. Cool on racks. Decorate with acrylic paint and glitter. *(Clay must be used within four hours or it will harden.)*

Cookie Cutter Cards

You will need:
- white and green construction paper
- Christmas cookie cutters
- poster paint (blue, green, red)
- pie tins
- construction paper and foil scraps
- paper punch
- ribbon
- glue
- pens and markers

Talk with your pastor about names and addresses of homebound members of your congregation and have individuals, families, or groups make and send them Christmas greetings.

Cut squares of white construction paper that are larger than your largest cookie cutter and punch a hole near one edge of each. Pour paint into pie tins. Dip a cookie cutter into the paint, shake off the excess, and press the outline firmly on a piece of white paper. When it dries, decorate with colored paper and foil scraps, markers, paints, and a Christmas message. Tie a loop of ribbon through the hole for hanging.

Angel Gift Bags

You will need:
- brown paper lunch bags (new or clean used ones)
- 6" or larger white paper doilies
- stapler
- glue
- scissors
- off-white and tan construction paper
- white and gold curly ribbon
- markers

Show how to use recycled or new lunch bags to make simple gift wrapping. Cut 2½" by 3" construction paper ovals and draw smiling angel faces on them. Fold a doily in half and glue a face on it as shown. Curl and cut short pieces of ribbon and glue them on the angel's head for hair. Put a small gift in the bag, fold down the open end evenly, and staple the doily over the top of the bag.

Suggest that the tops can be made ahead, and kept ready to close up bags as they are filled with gifts.

CELEBRATING CHRISTMAS

The "Las Posadas" procession might be used in conjunction with an intergenerational dinner gathering and brief candlelight worship service. The procession or the worship service may also be used for a church school opening worship. Caution is advised in using candles. The local fire chief should be consulted about your city's regulations.

' "Las Posadas," meaning "the inns," is a Mexican Christmas procession. A poor, bedraggled Mary and Joseph lead the procession to various places in the sanctuary or fellowship hall, singing a song asking for shelter at each place. At each place they are rejected by an innkeeper, until they reach an inn where they are allowed to use the manger.

The words to the following song may be photocopied for the participants and sung to the tune of "Good King Wenceslaus" as Mary and Joseph go from place to place. Joseph and Mary should be confident singers. Ask another strong singer to lead the rest of the participants.

Las Posadas Song

1 *(Joseph and Mary sing)*
In the name of God we beg: will you let us enter?
We are tired and we are cold. May we please have shelter?

(Innkeepers sing)
You look dirty and you smell. Will you please keep moving?
For your kind there is no place, for our inn is decent.

2 *(Joseph and Mary sing)*
It is not by our own choice that today we travel.
But the Emperor has said that all must be counted.

(Innkeepers sing)
For your reasons we care not. Every room is taken.
Can't you see the place is full? You are bad for business.

3 *(Joseph and Mary sing:)*
Will the child be born tonight out on a street corner?
Can't you find a place for him? Do you have no pity?

(Innkeepers sing)
Oh my goodness, do come in. You can use the manger.
For the rooms that we do have are for a rich traveler.

4 *(All sing)*
Holy Jesus, you are still with the poor and homeless;
If we wish to do your will, we will bid them welcome.

Holy Jesus, do forgive, in this Christmas season,
That the way in which we live, so beclouds our vision.
Amen.

This material is from *To Celebrate: Reshaping Holidays and Rites of Passage* published by Alternatives, P.O. Box 429, Ellenwood, GA 30049.

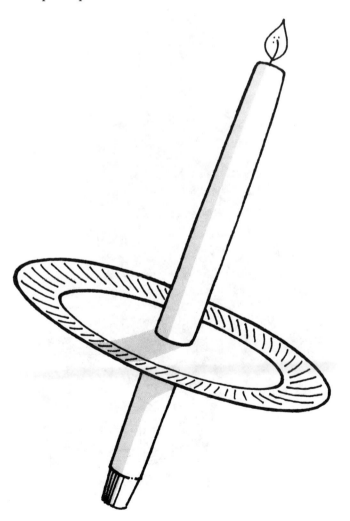

Gather everyone together around the holy family. Distribute candles. You may wish to have some shepherds arrive at the appropriate time in the scripture reading.

Scripture: Luke 2:1-20

Leader: *(The leader lights a candle.)* On Christmas Eve as we pass the flame from our candles, we share the light of Christmas with one another. Sharing this light makes more light and reminds us of the Christmas joy we can share with others throughout the year. *(Lights are dimmed and candles are lit one from another.)*

Leader: Let us pray. Emmanuel God, you come to us in this wonderful season of light in the gift of a little child. Help us to see you in the ordinary as well as the extraordinary things of life—in your word to us, in the care of a friend, and in the faces of those who need us. Amen.

Song: "Silent Night" or "Away in a Manger"

Benediction: May the Lord who has come to us as a little child bless us richly with his grace and keep us always in his light. Amen.

Christmas Love Tree

This may be an intergenerational event begun during Advent and used in conjunction with the Las Posadas service. Contact a community center, crisis shelter, care facility, or other institution to find out what guests or residents need, such as personal items, socks, or mittens. Find out whether items should be wrapped, and when and where they should be delivered.

Cut out simple construction paper tree ornaments, perhaps as a church school activity. On the back of each ornament, write one suggested gift. Put up a tree near the entrance to the sanctuary or in another prominent place. Place a large basket beneath it. Encourage members of the congregation to take home paper ornaments, bring back the appropriate gifts, and put them in the basket. You may want to wrap them with Angel Gift Bags or send Cookie Cutter Cards along with them.

EPIPHANY

THE SEASON OF LIGHT

Epiphany follows immediately after the 12 days of Christmas. The word *epiphany* means revelation or showing forth. God has appeared. God is revealed to the Magi as the child Jesus, and later as an adult when he is baptized, anointed with the Holy Spirit and called God's beloved Son.

Within these early stories of Jesus, the light of Christ shines. Jesus calls his followers like a prophet, has the power to turn water into wine, preaches the word of God with authority, heals the sick, and forgives sinners. In doing so, he shows God's power and mercy and explains God's word of hope and love and life. The season of Epiphany gives us a chance to explore this word, meant for us, through Christ. Like a light in the darkness, God's love surrounds us, challenges us, and directs us.

The day of Epiphany is best known for Matthew's story of the Magi, who followed the leading of a star. Matthew's Magi, or astrologers, came from different places some distance away. More than just observers of the stars, they studied the meaning of stars. Their beliefs were focused on the amazing heavens.

Modern astronomers tell us that at the time of Jesus' birth (probably about 6 B.C.), there was an extremely unusual and bright conjunction of the planets Jupiter and Saturn. Their combined light may well have been what the Magi followed to find the Christ.

Matthew's story calls Jesus' visitors "Magi" without specifying a number or gender. Tradition says Jesus was visited by three kings, perhaps because of the kingly gifts Jesus was given—gold, frankincense, and myrrh. Whatever the details, the story makes the point that God has been revealed to all the nations in Jesus.

A SYMBOL: THE STAR

The star is the symbol of Christ revealed, and of our journey with the Magi. During Epiphany we reflect upon being children of light. "This is the message we have heard from him and proclaim to you, that God is light and in him there is no darkness at all." (1 John 1:5 NRSV)

The colors of Epiphany are white and green. White indicates that The Epiphany of Our Lord and The Baptism of Our Lord are continuations of the joy of Jesus' birth. Jesus is discovered by the Magi and declared God's beloved child. Green suggests growth in the Spirit.

A SIGN: LIGHT

SONGS FOR EPIPHANY

"We Three Kings"
"Bright and Glorious Is the Sky"
"As with Gladness Men of Old"
"Morning Star, How Bright and Fair"

EPIPHANY ACTIVITIES

Epiphany Sand Star

You will need:
- lids from plastic five-quart ice cream tubs
- clean sand
- ball-shaped candles
- pencils
- ribbon scraps and bows from Christmas wrapping

Once Advent is passed, individuals, families, and groups can put together an alternative light source—an Epiphany sand star.

To make one star of light, spread a layer of clean sand inside a plastic ice cream lid. Evenly distribute five ball-shaped candles around the edge, pushing them securely into the sand. Position 10 pencils as shown to make the star points, and weave among them a colorful assortment of used ribbons and bows saved from Christmas wrappings.

Families may use the star as a table centerpiece to remind them of the sand through which the Magi traveled, the star that led the way, and the Christmas gift of Jesus.

When Epiphany is over, your church could collect the pencils and give them to a needy organization in your area, or send them with school kits to a mission area. (See Lutheran World Relief Kit information on this page.)

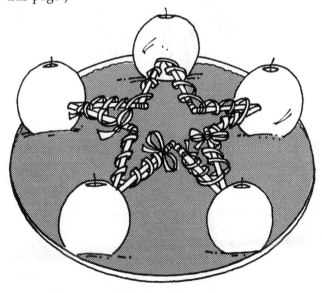

Starry Acts of Love

You will need:
- white construction paper
- string
- specific project information

In Matthew 5:16, Jesus says, "Let your light so shine before others that they may see your good works and give glory to God in heaven." Over the weeks of Epiphany, individuals, families, and other groups may plan and deliver gifts of light to meet needs in their local community and in the global community.

You might focus on a current event or participate in an ongoing church support project. Anything from a natural disaster to a new health clinic to serve a low-income neighborhood could benefit from your church's efforts. Lutheran World Relief and other global organizations have in place concrete ways to help people all around the world. One example is health kits. Participants collect items like bandages, combs, toothbrushes, and nail clippers that are sent to a central point for distribution near and far. Contact your local church's social service office or other agencies for details.

As each health kit or other project is completed, draw or write about it on a paper star. The stars are hung from the fellowship hall ceiling with string or displayed on a bulletin board. By the end of the Epiphany season, the room will be filled with "light."

Faith Journey Guidebooks

You will need:
- notebooks
- drawing tablets
- tape recorders
- blank cassette tapes
- video camera
- blank videotape

Make audiotapes and videotapes of people of all ages talking about their faith journeys. Some people may choose to record experiences on paper as they map their personal Epiphany journeys. Others will prefer to use more sophisticated equipment to record their reflections.

Suggest questions like these to stimulate thoughts and comments: When was God first revealed to you? Did you even realize it? When were you consciously aware of God's presence? What events along your life path have been challenges to you? Where do you experience God now? What is your God like? What does your understanding of God say about what believers are like?

Copies of these faith journeys guidebooks might be kept as references and sources of inspiration to pastors and other travel partners in your faith community.

CELEBRATING EPIPHANY

Preparation: *Plan the potluck meal. Make a star on a pole to lead the parade. Have a crèche set up in the sanctuary, and invite a storyteller in your church to tell the story of La Bafana. Use a children's picture book version of the story from your library to expand the short version below.*

On the weekend closest to Epiphany, try an intergenerational Epiphany celebration. Have a congregational potluck meal featuring foods light in color, texture, and weight. Encourage conversation about specific ways individuals, families, and groups within the congregation may lighten the burdens of people in crisis, either locally or in the broader community.

Follow the meal with a parade of "wise people," young and old, searching for the Christ child. All process to the sanctuary, singing Epiphany hymns and led by a glittering star on a pole. Festive accompaniment alternatives may be provided by kazoos, pans and spoons, horns and whistles.

Scripture: Matthew 2:1-15

Invite everyone to gather around the crèche as someone first reads the text from Matthew and then tells the story of La Bafana.

The story of La Bafana is an Italian legend of an old woman who is so busy cleaning her house that she misses the invitation of the Magi to join them in the search for the Christ child. Later, when she realizes her mistake, she runs to catch up with them. But she cannot. So she goes from door to door alone, searching for the child to whom she might give a gift. In her giving, she inadvertently finds the Christ child and serves him.

In Italy the story is celebrated by giving every child a small gift. Someone in the group might play La Bafana, walking among the gathered ones, looking for the Christ child and giving each child a small gift.

Song: "Bright and Glorious Is the Sky"

Blessing: May the one who revealed the Holy Child by the leading of a star lead you safely home to rest, guiding you in darkness and in light. Amen.

The Magi's Journey Game

See p. 62 for help to create this board game or floor game.

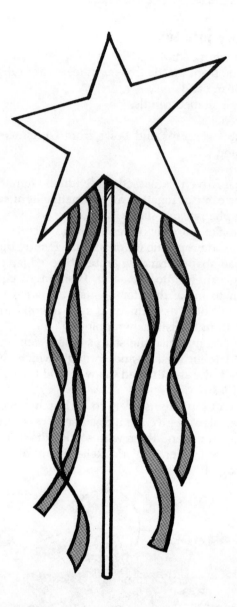

La Bafana Gifts

As a part of a churchwide Epiphany celebration or within Sunday school classrooms, La Bafana gifts may be made or bought and distributed to community children. Treats such as fruit or candy, along with small toys, are appropriate choices.

Tell the story of La Bafana below before beginning the activity. Explain that as we give to the needy people in the community, we seek and find the Christ child. Jesus says in Matthew 25:40 that as we serve others, we serve him.

LENT

THE SEASON OF SPRING

We begin the church year in Advent anticipating the birth of Christ. Then we celebrate the joy of Christmas and the light of Epiphany as God joins humanity and is revealed to us. Traditionally, Lent is a time of introspection, remembering, and repentance. We come face to face with our faults and realize that we must turn from them in order to have life, new life in Jesus.

At the same time that we look at our faults and needs, we anticipate Christ's death and resurrection. We repent, reorienting ourselves toward the one who took those faults into himself, thus fulfilling our deepest needs.

The word *Lent* means "spring." Lent functions within the church year as a springtime of the soul. In the spring we plan, clean out, and prepare our gardens for the growing season coming soon. We sort through clothes and household possessions, do major housecleaning, and open the windows to let in the fresh air.

In some Italian communities a bonfire marks the end of Epiphany and the beginning of Lent. People clean all the useless junk from their homes, pile it in the street, and set it afire. This cleaning out of the dead and useless to encourage the green of spring can spill out into our personal lives. We may also clean ourselves of the useless junk of greed, waste, and selfishness that go along with our lifestyles.

Traditionally, Lent was the time for new believers to give up their old ways and learn the faith so that they might be baptized on Easter Sunday.

Shrove Tuesday

Lent officially begins with Ash Wednesday. But the church has a long history of celebrating the day before, Shrove Tuesday. More popularly known by the French name, *Mardi Gras*, the name means "Fat Tuesday." Another variation is the Spanish *Carnival*, meaning "to take away meat." Both names suggest food, and traditional foods for Shrove Tuesday are rich and fatty. Shrove Tuesday is the day people used up the foods that would be forbidden during Lent. The day thus explores the indulgent side of human nature before the fasting and denial of Lent begin.

Shrove Tuesday is also a celebration of humor and foolishness before the seriousness and confession of Ash Wednesday. People dress up in costumes, paint their faces, and tease one another. They play noisemakers, beat on drums, and march in parades. The celebration ends on a serious note, however, in prayer and silence.

Ash Wednesday

Then comes Ash Wednesday. Participants in the Ash Wednesday service receive a cross of ashes on their foreheads. (The ash comes from the burning of palm fronds from the previous year's Passion Sunday celebration.) We remember how Christ was betrayed, how we betray others, and how our earthly bodies will betray us. We hear the words, "From dust you have come. To dust you shall return." We put on the ashes of mortality.

The 40 Days of Lent

The 40 days of Lent begin with Ash Wednesday, end with the Saturday before Easter, and exclude Sundays. On the Sundays of Lent we still celebrate the resurrection.

Lenten themes emphasize discipleship and spiritual renewal. Discipleship is, in part, a matter of self-understanding. As disciples, we are followers. Christian disciples are called to follow Jesus, God's Son. His life, his words, his involvement in our humanity shape us and free us to embrace the fullness of life promised by God by and measured against the one we follow, Jesus Christ.

Another piece of discipleship is commitment. Believers not only learn about Jesus; they encounter Jesus and are shaped by who he is. They are transformed; nothing is quite the same after we meet Jesus, the Christ. Our priorities realign; we see ourselves in a new way. God's love becomes the measure, and also our hope.

Christian love is powerful; it is neither simple nor sweet. Christian love is expressed most clearly in "God so loved the world that he gave his only Son, so that everyone who believes in him may not perish but may have eternal life" (John 3:16 NRSV). This is a love of sacrifice, a love that gives all. God offers what is most beloved—a part of self. Becoming disciples is a process of recognizing the love we receive and exploring the love we have to offer, including our whole selves.

Loving others as we love ourselves does not mean that we put on joyless, martyred faces. The Ash Wednesday gospel, Matthew 6:1-6, 16-21, tells us not to be hypocrites who give alms, fast, and pray so we might be admired or pitied. Such self-sacrifice is grim, troublesome, and ultimately selfish without love. But with love, giving is a joy. As disciples, we give of ourselves not for attention or to earn God's love and salvation. We love others, deeply and totally, because we recognize we were loved first. That love changes us forever, challenging us to grow. We are called into a process of becoming disciples, a process of spiritual renewal.

Believers experience God in creation, and in ongoing re-creation. In a sense, we are re-created every day when we awake. We are re-created in our baptism. During Lent we reflect on the fact that God comes to us and is present with us, daily creating a new heart in each of us.

The color used for Ash Wednesday is black, the color of the ashes. Purple may also be used. The color for Lent is purple, which reminds us of penitence.

A SYMBOL: THE CROSS

When Jesus broke bread with sinners (as he often did), he displayed radical love for the outsiders of his society. The bread that Jesus broke with his disciples on Maundy Thursday anticipated the breaking of his body that would happen the next day on the cross. The cross is the richest and most powerful of Christian symbols: it reminds us of God's love and Jesus' pain, but also of Jesus' resurrection. The empty cross is a statement of life. Love, the ultimate sacrifice, has conquered death, for us and for all people. The cross means we are free to begin again, to become what God intended us to be, to love.

The spiritual renewal that is central to Lent allows us to wear the cross as a symbol of our changed direction. Without counting the cost to ourselves, we turn with love and service toward God and our neighbors. We engage in lives of discipleship by facing death squarely and without fear. We know that, because we share in Jesus' death, we also share in his life. We celebrate the gift of life lived in a forgiven community. And we feel called to renewal with other disciples in the family of faith.

A SIGN: THE CROSS

SONGS FOR LENT

"All Glory, Laud, and Honor"
"Were You There"
"In the Cross of Christ I Glory"
"O Sacred Head, Now Wounded"
"Ride On, Ride On in Majesty"

LENT ACTIVITIES

A Spring Garden

You will need:
- white mural paper or newsprint
- masking tape or push-pins
- markers or crayons
- collage materials (optional)

Prepare ahead of time by beginning to draw a spring garden that the group will make to display along a hall or on a classroom bulletin board. Draw 10-20 fist-size or larger flower outlines on a strip of white mural paper or newsprint at least 3' x 5'. Leave plenty of space for people to add to the drawing with more flowers, grass, trees, and small animals.

Lent means "spring," the season of renewal, and it is time to be watching for signs of spring. We recognize spring outdoors in the new green of leaves and the pastels of flower buds. They emerge as pieces of God's plan, part of the ongoing cycle of creation.

We can watch for signs of God's kingdom coming all around us too. During Lent we open our eyes and our hearts to recognize signs of God's love.

People of all ages can appreciate that through acts of love and sacrifice, a garden of love emerges. Challenge individuals, families, and groups to recognize love people show to others during this season. Whenever you gather during Lent, talk together about acts of kindness you have witnessed, at home, at church, in the community, and even in the news. Draw or add color to something in the mural "garden" for each of those acts.

New Heart Pendant

During Lent we are spiritually renewed. God creates a new heart in each of us every day. Our new hearts are generous and kind; they reflect our new relationship with God, promised in Jeremiah 31:31-34. Although an exploration of this new heart could legitimately be tied to a celebration of Valentine's Day, emphasize that Christian love is more about an attitude and acts of love than about feelings of romance. Our new hearts remind us, too, that the reason we love is that we are first loved by God.

You will need:
- heart-shaped cookie cutters
- yarn of many colors, weights, and textures
- glue
- sturdy cardboard
- straight-edge blade or craft knife

Use a heart cookie cutter or stencil of your own design to determine the heart shape. Spread a layer of white glue all over one side of the heart, and then cover that glue entirely with yarn in decorative patterns, colors, and textures.

After the glue is dry, either use a glue gun to attach a safety pin to the back of the heart or make a necklace by looping a 24" piece of yarn through a hole you punch in the heart.

Prayer Tree

Lent is a time to cultivate a sense of concern for others as part of our own spiritual renewal. Invite members of your church to work together creating a prayer tree.

Set up a hallway bulletin board showing a large tree with many leafless branches or stand a large spring branch on a table in view of those coming to worship. Have slips of paper, pencils, and pins nearby, and also in the pews. Encourage church members to write short prayers or to ask for prayers for individuals as well as for peace, justice, and general concerns for others, and hang them on the tree. A filled branch is a beautiful reminder of the love you have for one another.

Whoever composes prayers for worship may incorporate some of these prayers. Be sure children have access to both the tree and the prayers.

Lenten Prayer Box

Lenten prayers may be composed and favorites recorded before meals and to begin each class during the season. These prayers may be written on slips of paper the first week of Lent and put in a shoe box decorated with praying hands, the names of participants, and Lenten symbols such as the cross, bread and wine, crown of thorns, and butterflies.

Boxes may be decorated for individuals, families, and groups to use at home and in other settings. Confirmation and other class boxes, as well as boxes for choirs, may be created with an appropriate focus in both the art and the prayers. Begin times to gather and times for individual devotions by picking out a prayer, praying it, and replacing it for use again.

Spring Cleaning

A church IS a presence in its community, whatever does or doesn't happen there. Your church can be a positive and faithful presence in your community by ACTING OUT its faith story and its values where all can witness it. Once your congregation understands Lent as a time for spring cleaning, dramatize Lent with some real spring cleaning.

Find out how a class, an intergenerational group, or the entire church school can help your church or community with a recycling or cleaning effort. Possibilities include: planting flowers, bushes, and ground cover around the church or at a local park; making and distributing containers for recyclable paper, aluminum cans, newspaper, and plastic; taking on a cleaning, repair, or painting job in a cellar, attic or storage area in a church or community building; and helping with a seasonal cleaning out of a local clothes closet.

Learning Faith with Mentors

Lent is a time for study of and reflection on the basics of faith. Early Christians spent the Lenten season learning about the faith in preparation for baptism on Easter morning.

Ask students about their baptismal sponsors. If they do not know who they were, have them ask their parents. Students might ask parents what they remember of their baptisms. Ask students to write about these special events. Students then may write a letter to their baptismal sponsors asking them about their faith and the most important thing that they think the student ought to know.

Because our society is so mobile, sponsors often live far away and have little immediate involvement with their godchildren. Meet the need for cross-generational contact with a mentoring program. Work with your pastor to match adult mentors from your congregation with high school and middle school youth. Arrange for pairs to meet twice during Lent. For each occasion, provide questions to stimulate discussion and space for both student and mentor to record responses, if they wish.

For the first meeting consider questions like these:

1. When and where were you baptized? How do you know about your baptismal day? Memories, photos, conversations with parents, sponsors, or others who were there?

2. Have you been confirmed? When and where? What do you remember about that day and the preparation for it?

3. What does your baptism mean to you?

4. What does your confirmation mean to you?

5. What would you tell someone about to be baptized?

6. What would you tell someone about to be confirmed?

When you finish, pray the Lord's Prayer together.

For the second meeting suggest questions like these:

1. Who has been an influential person in your life of faith? Why?

2. What would the best possible life be like? What would the worst be?

3. What or who helps you most when you are in trouble?

When you finish, pray the Lord's Prayer together.

CELEBRATING LENT

Shrove Tuesday Celebration

Preparation: Paint a large ALLELUIA on a piece of newsprint before the celebration. Make arrangements for the potluck, games, and prizes.

Shrove Tuesday is an excellent time to have an intergenerational event. It might be more easily celebrated the weekend before Ash Wednesday, when there is more time to prepare than a weeknight. Traditional food for the celebration is made with fat, since Christians tried to use up all the fat in the house before Lent, when it was forbidden to eat fat. A potluck of everyone's favorite desserts would be a great way to start a Shrove Tuesday celebration. You might also have pancakes, donuts, or other foods made with fats.

Everyone should be encouraged to come in masks or costumes. Someone could paint faces with theater makeup at the door, or masks could also be available at the door for those who come without. Give prizes for the best, most original, and silliest costumes or masks.

Plan games such as bingo and a luggage relay, in which participants run to suitcases of large, silly clothing that must be put on and taken off before they tag the next person. Have skits, upbeat music, and candy for everyone.

Hand out noisemakers, drums, or pots and pans. End the celebration with a noisy parade to the sanctuary for a service of prayer.

Once in the sanctuary, observe a time of silence as we remember the part of us that we want to put away during Lent. We confess our sins and pray as a community that God will transform us during the Lenten season. You may wish to use the rite for confession from your church's worship book or a confession such as Psalm 51. Sing "Create in Me a Clean Heart" or a similar hymn of confession and renewal.

Explain that it is time to "put away the Alleluia for the season." Point to the large, colorful ALLELUIA you prepared and displayed. Be sure everyone understands that the word is an expression of praise or thanksgiving. Ask children to come forward, fold up the paper, and put it in a box. Explain that it will not come out again until Easter. Leave in silence. Try to clean up in silence, as well. You will be surprised at how effectively this event prepares people for Ash Wednesday.

Lenten Worship

The following short services may be used for Sunday school openings during Lent. They highlight the 40 days of Lent by telling several "40-day stories" from the Bible.

WEEK 1: NOAH

Leader: This is the first week of Lent, a time when we think about discipleship and spiritual renewal. There are 40 days in Lent. When we gather during these 40 days, we will hear Bible stories about people who experienced God in a special way over another 40 days. All of these people learn how much God loves us and wants us to love one another. The first story is about God saving Noah from the flood. Do you remember what sign God gave to Noah? (*The rainbow.*)

Scripture: Genesis 7:1, 13-17

Prayer: O God, like Noah, we have things that seem ready to drown us, to overpower us. You saved us in the water of our baptism. Thank you for your love. Amen.

Benediction: May the God who saved Noah from the waters of the flood keep you every day. Go in peace. Serve the Lord.
All: Thanks be to God.

WEEK 2: MOSES

Leader: This second week in Lent, we remember the prophet who brought the Ten Commandments down from the mountain of God. Moses spent 40 days on the mountain with God. The Ten Commandments were given to the people to help them love God and one another. The first three commandments tell us to love God. The other seven guide us in our love for one another. Listen to the story.

Scripture: Exodus 24:12-18

Prayer: O God, guide our actions toward love for you, each other, and all creation. Amen.

Benediction: May the God who gave Moses the Ten Commandments direct your thoughts and actions toward love for one another. Go in peace. Serve the Lord.
All: Thanks be to God.

WEEK 3: ELIJAH

Prepare for this dramatic presentation of 1 Kings 19:1-18 by printing each of the following on one 9" x 12" sheet of construction paper: "P"; "CCC"; "SH"; and "O." Choose instrumentalists to play a triangle and a rattle, and choose readers for the parts of the narrator, God, and Elijah.

Leader: Our 40 days story for the third week of Lent is about Elijah, and all of you are going to help tell it. When you see "P," please pat your laps. That will be Elijah running. When you see "O," say "O" to sound like a great wind. When you see "CCC," clap three times. That will be the sound of an earthquake. When you see "SH," say a long "SHHH" to sound like a big fire. (*Have someone point to letter signs and musicians as needed to signal group participation with readers*).

Narrator: Once upon a time, in the old land of Israel, there was a prophet of God named Elijah. King Ahab and Queen Jezebel hated Elijah. They threatened to kill him.
So Elijah ran away from the evil king and queen. *[P]* He was very afraid. He was so afraid that he prayed to God to take away his life. An angel *[triangle]* came and gave Elijah special food. It was heavenly *[triangle]* food, and it gave him the strength to travel for 40 days to Mount Horeb, the mountain of God. There Elijah spoke with God. *[rattle]*

God: What are you doing here, Elijah?

Elijah: I have been very faithful. I have loved only you. I have been against all those who hate you. But now I am the only faithful one left. And the king and queen are trying to kill me. *[rattle]*

God: Go and stand on the mountain. I am about to pass by.

Narrator: So Elijah stood out on the mountain. And there was a great wind. *[O]* But God was not in the wind. Next there was an earthquake. *[CCC]* But God was not in the earthquake. Then there was a fire. *[SH]* But God was not in the fire. Finally there was silence, and a still, small voice. *[rattle]*

God: Elijah, do not be afraid. You are not alone. There are 7000 faithful people in Israel. And I will give you a helper. His name is Elisha.

Narrator: And Elijah knew that he was not alone. So Elijah went and found Elisha, who became his helper.

Prayer: O God, sometimes as we help others we become discouraged and afraid. Feed us, too, with your heavenly food. Help us trust you when we need help and encouragement. Amen.

Benediction: May the God who spoke to Elijah in a quiet voice when he was afraid come to us and give us peace. Go in peace. Serve the Lord.
All: Thanks be to God.

WEEK 4: JONAH
Leader: This is the fourth week in Lent, a time when we think about living as God would like us to live, loving God and others. How many days are there in the season of Lent? *(40)* During Lent we have been learning about Bible people who experienced God in a special way during 40 days—so far, Elijah, Moses, and Noah. Today we hear the story of another person from the Bible who learned about God's love. At first, Jonah thought God loved only those who were good.

JONAH RAP
(Ask someone to play a drum or other percussion instrument in rhythm. The capitals designate the stressed beats.)

1. Oh, the WORD of the LORD came to OUR man JOnah
Saying, "GET on BOARD a MIGHty SHIP,
And GO at ONCE to NINeVEH, to NINeVEH, to NINeVEH.
GO at ONCE to NINeVEH, and SAVE the PEOple THERE. GO!"

2. When JOnah HEARD the WORD of the LORD
He RAN aWAY as FAST as he COULD.
He RAN aWAY from NINeVEH, from NINeVEH, from NINeVEH,
He RAN aWAY from NINeVEH, and said to God, "NO!"

3. "I WON'T help FOLKS in NINeVEH, in NINeVEH, in NINeVEH.
They're WICKed, RUDE, and MEAN,
from EV'ryTHING I've SEEN."
But GOD sent SOMEthing GREEN . . . a FISH went SWISH and SWALLowed JOnah, SWALLowed JOnah DOWN.

4. JO found himSELF on SHORE
(the FISH showed HIM the DOOR),
and THAT was ALL it TOOK—
Jo HAD to TAKE a LOOK
at ALL the FOLKS in NINeVEH, in NINeVEH, in NINeVEH.
He SAW them THROUGH God's EYES.
And THAT was A surPRISE!

5. You KNOW what JOnah DID? He LOOKED.
You KNOW what JOnah DID? He THOUGHT.
Then he TOLD the FOLKS in NINeVEH, in NINeVEH, in NINeVEH,
he TOLD the FOLKS in NINeVEH exactly what God said:
"You've GOT just FORty DAYS
to STOP and CHANGE your WAYS."
AND THEY DID!
God was RIGHT to send JOnah THERE.

Prayer: O God, you love and care for all you create. Thank you for helping us love and care for one another, near and far. Amen.

Benediction: May the God who sent Jonah to warn the people of Nineveh, send us in love to the world. Go in peace. Serve the Lord.
All: Thanks be to God.

WEEK 5: JESUS
Leader: This is the last week in Lent. How many days are there in the season of Lent? *(40)* Remember that the 40-day stories of Elijah, Moses, Noah, and Jonah were all about God's love. Today's story is about God's love, too. We learn best about God's love by learning about Jesus.

In today's story, Jesus goes into the wilderness for 40 days to pray right after he is baptized. While he is there, the devil tempts him to love and help only himself. But Jesus already knows what he must do—he must show God's love to all the world by dying on the cross and rising again to save us.

Scripture: Matthew 3:16—4:11

Prayer: Thank you, God, for sending Jesus. How much you must love us that you would give everything for us, even your Son. Amen.

Benediction: May the God who sent us our savior Jesus send us in love to the world, and give us peace. Go in peace. Serve the Lord.
All: Thanks be to God.

LEARNING ABOUT HOLY WEEK

On one level, Holy Week is simply the last seven of the 40 days of Lent. On another level, the events of Holy Week tell the whole story of the Christian faith. So much happens in this one week as day by day we observe the passion of Christ!

Palm Sunday

Holy Week begins on the Sunday before Easter, called Palm Sunday and also called Passion Sunday. On the first Palm Sunday, the people celebrated Jesus the king. As he rode into Jerusalem on a donkey, they remembered the Old Testament promise of the Messiah coming just that way, in Zechariah 9:9. But when he did not show his power in the way they thought he should, their "Hosannas!" ended.

Maundy Thursday

The next dramatic event of what we call Holy Week was the meal that Jesus and his disciples shared. They ate the Passover meal together on Maundy Thursday. Along with other Jews, then and now, they celebrated in the Passover the freeing of their Israelite ancestors from slavery to the Egyptians. An introduction to the Passover meal, or Seder, as it might be celebrated among Jewish people today is found on page 36.

Seemingly unaware of the radical importance of the experience, in this final meal with Jesus the disciples were given a glimpse of the kingdom of God, a foretaste of the feast to come. *Maundy* means "command." At that meal, Jesus demonstrated perfect service and love. He washed their feet. On Maundy Thursday, Jesus gave his disciples, and all those who have followed through the centuries, the commands to remember him in bread and wine and to love one another. He also acknowledged his betrayal was imminent.

At the end of traditional Maundy Thursday services, Psalm 22 may be read and the altar stripped in silence. The haunting notion of betrayal leads the penitent Christian from the loving service of Maundy Thursday into its result on Good Friday.

Good Friday

Good Friday is for Christians the official bad day of the year. It is the day when the evil of the world is most solemnly and bleakly portrayed. On this day, evil seemed to triumph. Our Lord died, and somehow we feel a part of that betrayal and death long ago.

There is a season even for grief. There are times when life is difficult and evil seems to win the day. Sometimes when we have no words for our own grief and loss, the symbols of faith and the presence of our community provide them.

An example: A young woman's friend dies suddenly. He also was young and his death seems meaningless. She feels she can no longer believe in a gracious God. She stops attending worship—but she feels guilty for not attending.

One Sunday she drags herself to church. The liturgy, which had always given her solace, is her enemy. She feels cynical as she sits silently through hymns, readings, and the sermon. But as the congregation begins to pray she begins to feel something else. They pray for her. They express her grief and, miraculously, her gratitude. They weep for her. They present her case—against an evil world—to God. She has no words. The community has them for her.

Our personal Good Fridays might not be such bad days, but each year Good Friday worship is an occasion to remember the evil of the world. The altar is bare and we extinguish light, the symbol of the life of Christ. By dying on a cross and rising again, Jesus has defeated sin and evil and even death. Because we, as members of the Christian community, confront the reality of Jesus' death on Good Friday, we are able to proclaim Christ's victory on Easter Sunday.

Traditionally, the colors of Holy Week are red, the color of blood, or purple, signifying both royalty and repentance. Some churches use white on Maundy Thursday because we remember the Lord's Supper, and white is traditionally associated with the festivals of Christ. In many churches, there are no paraments, banners, or other decorative items out on Good Friday. They are removed on Maundy Thursday and not replaced until Easter Sunday. The color of the day for Good Friday is red, or black, the color of mourning.

HOLY WEEK ACTIVITIES

Dramatizing Passion Sunday Texts

Students may act out the long Passion Sunday texts (Matthew 26:1-27, 66; or Mark 14:1-15, 47; or Luke 22:1-23, 56). Prepare scripts that match the talents of the people who will perform. Choose one or more narrators and individuals to be such lead characters as Jesus and Pilate. Those who don't want parts can be the crowd. Assemble costumes and props, if possible. Allow plenty of time to practice parts. Arrange to dramatize the text for the Passion Sunday worship or for Sunday school opening worship.

Freeze Frame

With a smaller group, you may also wish to "freeze frame" the text. Choose a narrator to read small portions of text at a time as the rest of the group silently "freezes" in certain positions that capture the text. For example, as Luke 23:32-38 is read, one person may stand with arms outstretched, one may kneel with a hand outstretched as though casting lots, several may kneel and watch with interest while others stand back and point. With each portion of text, or at specified points, the scene shifts. Participants of all ages will enjoy helping decide how each person can contribute to their "snapshot" of the story.

Where Is Jesus Today?

Take a group or class on a tour around your community to consider where people experience Jesus' love and care today. Some places you might visit would be a neighboring church, a school, a hospital, a house built by Habitat for Humanity, a shelter for people who are homeless, a counseling center, and a food or clothing distribution outlet. You may wish to carry a cross and read from the Passion Sunday gospel text at each place.

A Walk Through Holy Week

Let individuals, families, and groups make Holy Week strips with symbols that will remind them of the events of Holy Week. Provide long strips in a variety of materials of different sizes on which people may chart the events of Holy Week with simple symbols. Include the following events in order, but without the day designations. Expect some illustrations to include great detail and others to be very simple. Affirm them all.

1. A palm to remind us of Jesus' triumphant entry into Jerusalem.

2. A bag of coins to remind us that Jesus was betrayed by one of his friends.

3. A bowl of water and towel to remind us that Jesus taught us to love one another by washing his disciples' feet.

4. Wine and bread to remind us of Jesus' last meal with the disciples.

5. A rooster to remind us that all the disciples finally left Jesus before the rooster crowed three times.

6. A cross to remind us of Jesus' suffering.

7. The tomb with the stone rolled in front of the opening to remind us that Jesus died.

8. A butterfly to remind us that Jesus was raised from the dead and lives forever.

Paradise Torte

This Easter cake is traditionally baked three days before Easter, in order to be ready to be eaten on Easter.

To make the cake layers:

Grease and flour four round 9″ cake pans. Preheat oven to 350 degrees.

1 cup butter or margarine
2 cups sugar
1 whole egg
4 egg yolks (save the whites)
½ teaspoon salt
1 lemon rind, grated
3 cups flour

Cream butter and sugar. Add eggs, salt, and lemon rind. Work in flour. Dough will be stiff. Divide dough into four equal portions and pat into prepared pans making thin layers.

To make the topping:

4 egg whites
¾ cup sugar
½ pound almond paste, grated
1 teaspoon cinnamon

Beat egg whites until soft peaks form. Fold into the egg whites, the grated almond paste, sugar and cinnamon. Divide mixture into four equal portions and spread on top of each layer. Bake the layers for 25-35 minutes or until the cakes are a rich golden brown. Cool slightly but remove from pans while still warm. The layers come out of the pan as crisp, round disks.

Before assembling the cake:

Beat 1 pint of whipping cream until thick, and choose the cake layer with the most perfect bottom and have it ready to be inverted to become the top of the cake.

To assemble the cake:

Begin with one cake layer on a plate and spread one-third of the whipped cream over it. Add the remaining layers and cream, ending with the best cake layer inverted on top. Allow the whipped cream to ooze out between the layers somewhat by pressing gently on the top of the cake. You may spread excess cream around the sides of the cake and sprinkle almond slivers on the cream.

Keep the torte in a cool place (not the refrigerator) for about three days. Check the torte daily. The temperature and weather affect how long it will take for the torte to "ripen." When it is soft and settled, put it in the refrigerator.

To serve, decorate the top with a sprinkling of powdered sugar. A paper stencil or lace doily design can be created with the powdered sugar. Cut this rich dessert into small slices.

The Seder:
Introducing a Passover Meal

Note: In order to show respect to the Jewish people and their faith, it is critical that we not try to imitate the Seder, turning it into a prelude to the New Testament Lord's Supper. If your church wishes to participate in an authentic Seder, ask a rabbi in your community to help you.

The History

The gospels tell us that Jesus' last meal with his disciples was a Passover meal. Christians may be interested in Passover because it celebrates an important part of the salvation history we share with our Jewish sisters and brothers. Also, our understanding of Passover and the Seder can enrich our understanding of the events of Holy Week.

The Seder takes place on the first evening of the week-long celebration of Passover which recalls God's deliverance of the Israelites from their Egyptian masters. The climax of the story is found in Exodus 12–15. The angel of death God sent to kill every firstborn in Egypt "passed over" the homes of Israelites because God had instructed them to put lamb's blood over their doors.

The Seder, a contemporary, not biblical reenactment of the meal, is not typically celebrated in public worship places such as synagogues. Rather, it is celebrated in Jewish homes, as it was celebrated the first time in Egypt.

The Preparations

Homes are prepared for Passover with a thorough "spring housecleaning." Special utensils and dishes are used. Leavened food such as bread, crackers, and breakfast cereals are put away as a reminder of the unleavened bread the escaping Israelites had to eat. (There was no time for them to let their dough rise.) No bread at all, not even matzoh, is eaten for a full day before the Passover meal.

Traditionally, the night before the Passover celebration begins, children enjoy the ceremony of B'dikat Hametz, meaning "searching for leaven." A parent hides pieces of bread wrapped in paper around the home. Children search for them in the dark with a flashlight.

The table is set beautifully for the Passover Seder, with special dishes and candles. An empty chair is left as a reminder of those who are oppressed or imprisoned, or who are not free to celebrate the Passover. A particularly beautiful cup is set on the table for the prophet Elijah. At a dramatic moment during the evening, children open the door for Elijah.

The Food and its Significance

Note: Cookbooks with recipes for the Seder meal are available. Work with a local rabbi on the preparation of the following items, if you will be tasting them as part of a Seder.

On the plate of the leader and on serving dishes around the table are the matzoh, parsley, the top of a horseradish root, and charoset. A cup for wine is by each place as well. The leader's plate also holds a roasted lamb shankbone and a roasted egg; other participants have bowls of salt water by their places.

- Matzoh is an unleavened cracker-like bread, a reminder of the Israelites' hasty escape from Egypt.
- Wine (or grape juice) is the fruit of the vine, which represents the promises of God the creator.
- A well-roasted shankbone of lamb reminds us of the Paschal lamb, which was sacrificed at the temple in Jerusalem on Passover long ago.
- A roasted egg is a reminder of the second offering brought to the temple for Passover.
- Parsley (and other greens) are reminders of the rebirth and renewal of spring. They are to be dipped in salty water and eaten.
- Salty water is a reminder of the tears of the Israelite slaves. Parsley or other greens are to be dipped in dishes of the water and eaten.
- Horseradish (the maror) symbolizes the bitterness that the Israelites experienced in Egypt, and the lot of all who are oppressed or enslaved today.
- Charoset is a combination of finely chopped apple, chopped walnuts or pecans, and mashed raisins, dates, prunes, or apricots, with cinnamon and wine to taste. It is the color of the mortar that held together the bricks the Israelite slaves were forced to make, and is eaten between two pieces of matzoh.

The Service

Note: Learning about the Seder will be most positive and respectful when it is done with a local rabbi.

The leader reviews the story of the Passover with readings, songs, and questions from children about the significance of the night.

Seder participants remember that breaking bread binds all people together and redemption comes with the deliverance of all people from bondage. The last thing eaten is a piece of matzoh, a taste of freedom. Among the texts read during the Seder are Psalms 113, 114, and 126; Exodus 12–20; and Numbers 9:11.

EASTER

THE SEASON OF NEW LIFE

The resurrection of Jesus of Nazareth is the single most important event on the Christian calendar. Early in the morning, the women found the tomb empty and ran to the others with the cry, "He is risen!" On Easter morning we respond to their joy once more. To their story we add our own stories of faith and reply, "He is risen indeed!"

Some churches begin the Easter celebration in the pre-dawn darkness, and celebrate the rising of the light of the world from the dead, as the sun symbolically rises over the earth.

Two thousand years earlier, Christians met just before Easter daybreak in a cistern, an underground storage place for water. As the sound of running water echoed up the cavernous, stony sides, baptismal candidates oiled their bodies and renounced the power of Satan in their lives. When a rooster crowed, announcing the light of a new day, a deacon brought candidates into the bubbling, flowing water. They were immersed three times as they responded to a portion of a trinitarian creed. Once again they were anointed with oil, this time with blessings and thanksgiving. They were clothed in baptismal robes and led to another room where other Christians greeted them. There they shared the Lord's Supper. The newly baptized also drank a cup of milk and honey signifying their entrance into the promised land.

Christians today often celebrate Easter with a new outfit, much as the early Christians put on their white robes, to signify a new life. New clothing can recall the baptismal robes of Easter. As believers we shed the old life, putting on Christ and his resurrection.

A story is told of Dorothy Day, a Christian reformer in the early 20th century, who helped people who were homeless in New York City. At Easter she had only a little change in her pocket to buy some new item of clothing and celebrate the new life of the resurrection. She bought new shoelaces. Even new shoelaces can signify the hope and promise of Easter.

Philippine families gather to celebrate the new life of Easter and offer symbols of new life—plants, seeds, eggs, butterflies, even booties—and hang them on an Easter tree. Children everywhere plant seeds and give and receive gifts of eggs, sweets, and special foods.

Every Sunday is an Easter celebration. But Easter morning and the Sundays of the Easter season especially celebrate the power of the resurrection to put on the new. The Epistle texts follow the story of the beginnings of the church in the book of Acts. Peter preaches with power, and thousands are converted. When the disciples are imprisoned, their jailors fall asleep, only to wake in an empty jail.

The disciples seem almost as amazed as the local officials. Philip baptizes an Ethiopian and the story of God's love and Jesus' resurrection spreads. Even the mean and violent Saul puts on new life. He has a life-changing experience on the road to Damascus, and his ministry as the apostle Paul begins.

In our worship, light, which grew during the season of Advent on the wreath and was taken away at the end of the Maundy Thursday service, is rekindled along with new life. The sanctuary is alive with flowers. The alleluias return and are repeated over and over. The ashes of Lent are washed away with the water of new life, and people are clothed in their best. We are renewed.

The color for Easter is white, because it celebrates one of the major events in the life of Christ. Gold is also proper because it is the most holy day of the church year.

A SYMBOL: THE EGG

Eggs have long symbolized breaking out of bondage to new life. Egyptians and Germans put an egg in the tomb or grave with the dead. Greeks still decorate their loved ones' graves with painted eggs. Ukrainians, using hot wax, dyes and fine tools, elevated the painting of eggs to an art form. Some people cut branches from bushes or trees that are well budded and put them in a vase of water. They blow out eggs, decorate them and tie them on the branch. Over the first few days of Easter, the branch begins to leaf out, and a tree, which once held the dying Savior, signals new life.

Some Hungarian boys go from house to house on Easter Monday, and wherever girls live, recite a blessing and splash the girls with water, reminding them of new life in Christ. The girls invite them in, give them some beautiful eggs to take home with them, and everyone eats Easter goodies. The girls do the same for the boys on Easter Tuesday.

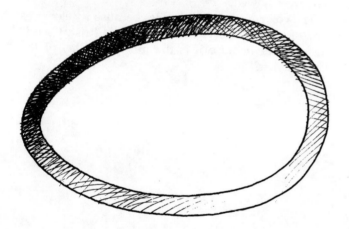

A SIGN: THE BUTTERFLY

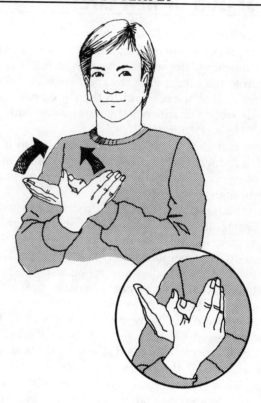

SONGS FOR EASTER

"Christ the Lord Is Ris'n Today; Alleluia!"
"The Strife Is O'er, the Battle Done"
"Now All the Vault of Heav'n Resounds"
"Thine Is the Glory"

EASTER ACTIVITIES

Coloring Easter Eggs

You will need:
- hardboiled eggs
- crayons and markers
- commercial egg dye materials
- red and yellow onion skins
- leaves or herbs
- old nylon stockings

Note: If the eggs will NOT be eaten, you may also use bleach and toothpicks, tissue paper and wallpaper paste, and clear fingernail polish, either for decorating or for bonding the decorations. If you would like to keep the eggs you decorate for an extended period of time, you must remove the yolk and the white. To blow out an egg, use a pin to poke a small hole in the narrow end of the egg. On the opposite end, make a larger hole. Blow through the smaller hole into a bowl. Rinse the egg thoroughly and dry it in the carton, large hole down.

Try one or more of the following techniques for coloring eggs. Gear the options to the space and equipment you have, and also to the skill levels of participants. As individuals, families, and groups do their eggs, encourage conversations about the egg as an Easter symbol.

- Use light-colored or white crayons to put messages or symbols on eggs. Then dye with commercial dyes made specifically for eggs. Areas with crayon wax will not absorb the dye.
- Older children and adults may dye the eggs first and then, using a toothpick, bleach designs on them.
- Poster paints make bright eggs. Be generous with the paint. When dry, apply clear polish.
- Tear or cut tissue paper into 1" pieces. Brush glue on the egg, then smooth on the paper. Try overlapping several colors and creating interesting textures.
- Add subtle, natural colors to eggs by boiling them inside an old nylon stocking with onion skins, beet slices, and bright leaves or herbs. Tie tightly with bread bag ties. Remove and let dry.

- Create a multicolored egg with three dips into the three primary colors—red, yellow, and blue. Step 1: Dip the narrow end half of the egg into red egg dye. Step 2: Dip the wide end half of the egg into yellow egg dye. Step 3: Dip one half of the egg held sideways into blue egg dye. Dry after each step.

Forcing Bulbs

You will need:
- white flower bulbs
- potting soil
- plant pots

Plant bulbs with the tops just showing above the soil. Allow four weeks for blooms. Take them to homebound friends to remind them of new life.

Sandpaper Butterflies

You will need:
- coarse sandpaper
- crayons
- white construction paper
- iron
- newspapers

Butterflies, typically light and airy, take on a different look and feel when they are made using sandpaper.

On the rough side of the sandpaper, use crayons to color a bright butterfly. Be sure there is a thick layer of crayon. Put a piece of white paper on several layers of newspaper. Then position the sandpaper, colored side down, on the white paper. Iron the sandpaper back through at least two layers of newspaper, at a medium setting.

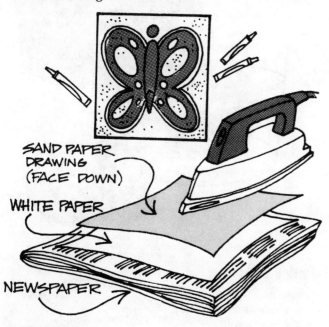

SAND PAPER DRAWING (FACE DOWN)

WHITE PAPER

NEWSPAPER

New Shoelaces

Many families do not have the resources for new clothing at Easter. Publicize the need for contributions to a local clothing exchange or distribution center using the story of Dorothy Day on page 37. Even those who are concerned about people in need can forget to donate regularly. By asking for something as unusual as shoelaces, you may elicit quite a response. Advertise for laces of many sizes and colors with imaginative posters that you can display in your church and around the community.

You might also suggest that church school offerings be designated for new clothes for a needy neighborhood family.

A Walk to Water

Take a group or class on a walk to the nearest lake, river, ocean, or puddle. As you go, tell the Bible story of Philip and the Ethiopian in Acts 8:26-40. On his walk, Philip met someone he didn't expect to meet (but that God sent to meet him). They rode together in the man's carriage while Philip told him the story of Jesus and the resurrection. When the man saw water, he asked Philip to baptize him. Philip did.

Talk about water as a continuing sign of God's presence and life renewed among us. If you wait to take this walk until the first signs of spring appear in your area, you could splash a little water, a life blessing, on each person, as a reminder of their baptisms. Feed the birds, and observe all living things around you.

Easter Tree

You will need:
- budded branch (forsythia works well)
- eggs, blown out and decorated
- paper
- people, butterfly, and flower shapes or stencils
- markers
- string

An Easter tree can be a cheery reminder of the new life of Jesus and the new life of spring.

Keep the branch cutting moist until you can put it into a vase of water. Provide paper so that individuals, families, and groups can cut shapes of people, butterflies, flowers, and other signs of new life. Suggest that individuals color people to look like themselves, since they also have new life in Christ. Use string to hang egg and paper treasures of new life on the "tree," as you would on a Christmas tree. Branches will leaf out in a few days.

CELEBRATING EASTER

Easter Vigil: A Service of Light

Preparation: Work with your pastor to plan the service for your congregation. Choose assistants for the liturgy at the beginning and to read the lessons. Have a small candle for each participant, a large white candle set in a stand in front of the altar, a pine bough, and a bowl of water.

What follows is a simplified Easter Vigil service intended for use by an intergenerational group the Saturday evening before Easter. The procession and the use of light and water will engage participants of all ages in the mysteries of Easter in a powerful way. The vigil might be followed by a simple shared meal and some songs of hope.

Begin with the sanctuary as dark as possible. Have people gather outdoors or outside the sanctuary as the large candle is lighted.

Leader 1: May the light of Christ fill the darkness of our hearts and minds.
Leader 2: *(lifting the candle)* The light of Christ.
All: Thanks be to God!

Each person lights her or his small candle from the large candle. Then Leader 2 leads the procession into the sanctuary, stops before the altar, and turns to face the participants. After all reach their places, Leader 2 lifts the candle high.

Leader 1: The light of Christ.
All: Thanks be to God!
Leader 2: Through the darkness of this night we begin to see a light—and we rejoice.
Leader 1: Through the darkness of this earth the church feels a new birth and sees a light—and we rejoice.
Leader 2: The brightness spreads, shouts of joy resound, the triumphant voices of the people.
Leader 1: Long ago you brought salvation from the land of Egypt to your people, the children of Israel.
Leader 2: Long ago you brought salvation from evil and the gloom of sin to us, believers in Christ.
Leader 1: Long ago, in a night dark as this, Christ broke the chains of death, securing our freedom from hell and despair.
Leader 2: We pray, O God, that your Son Jesus, whose light we mirror with these candles, will continue to end this night's darkness and light our way to faithfulness. Amen.

(Participants extinguish their candles and are seated. Enough lights may be turned on in the sanctuary so that participants may read.)

First Lesson

Reader 1: A reading from Genesis 1:1-5.
Pastor: Let us pray. Almighty God, you wonderfully created the dignity of human nature and yet more wonderfully restored it. In your mercy, let us share his divine life, Jesus Christ. Amen.

Second Lesson

Reader 2: A reading from Genesis 22:1-18.
Pastor: Let us pray. God of all the faithful, you promised Abraham and Sarah that you would make their descendants like the grains of sand. Help us to respond to your call by joyfully accepting our new life of grace, through Jesus Christ. Amen.

Third Lesson

Reader 3: A reading from Exodus 14:10-14, 21-25.
Pastor: Let us pray. O God, by the power of your mighty arm you delivered the children of Israel from slavery, a sign for us that you save all the nations by the water of baptism, through Jesus Christ. Amen.

Fourth Lesson

Reader 4: A reading from Daniel 3:1-2, 23-27.
Pastor: Holy God, hear us as we confess our faith in you. *(Use a confession of faith from your church's worship book. Three times, once with each portion of the creed, the pastor dips the pine bough in the water and sprinkles it over the congregation.)*
Pastor: You have made public confession of your faith. Do you intend to continue in the covenant God made with you in Holy Baptism: to live among God's faithful people, to hear God's Word and share in the Lord's Supper, to proclaim the good news of God in Christ through word and deed, to serve all people, following the example of our Lord Jesus, and to strive for justice and peace in all the earth?
All: We do, with God's help and guidance. *(Participants leave in silence.)*

The Easter ALLELUIA

Easter morning worship can begin powerfully with the bringing out of the ALLELUIA. Ask the children who helped pack away the large ALLELUIA on newsprint for Lent to come up, take it out of the box, and unfold it. Ask when they last saw it, and how it felt to pack it away. Talk about taking it out and the joy of Jesus' resurrection.

Use the ALLELUIA by singing a favorite Easter hymn that has lots of "Alleluias" in it. There should be many "Alleluias" on Easter!

PENTECOST

THE SEASON OF THE HOLY SPIRIT

Shortly after Jesus' resurrection and ascension, people were still gathered in Jerusalem for the Passover celebration. On the last day of that celebration, the disciples were gathered together in one place. On that day of Pentecost the world as it was known ended, and a new world began. The Holy Spirit came among them suddenly like wind and fire, powerful and frightening. Those who were celebrating the Passover were amazed as they heard the disciples speaking in their own languages.

The Day of Pentecost is the time when we pray for clarity, the opposite of the confusion created with the Tower of Babel in Genesis 11. Our differences with others near and far have been overcome by the power of the Holy Spirit, and point us toward God's message of love, freedom and salvation for all creation. Therefore it is a day when we strive for understanding and community with our neighbors.

The Sundays after Pentecost are a time when we remember the life of the Church. The season begins with the life and teachings of Jesus and ends with looking forward to the last times, the end of the world. In the meantime we celebrate life together in God's Spirit. Life without the Spirit is shallow and self-serving. Life in the Spirit is different. In baptism, the Spirit claims us, transforms us, makes us one in Christ, and activates our gifts in service. The Spirit inspires our intentions and attitudes.

The Spirit inspires our faith over and over again, pointing us always to God. Martin Luther puts it this way: "I believe that I cannot by my own understanding or strength believe in Jesus Christ my Lord or come to him." We know that we are sinners who try to control everything, who rebel against being human. But the Holy Spirit keeps us in the one true faith. We continue to say, "I can't believe this." The Holy Spirit helps us say, "I believe because Jesus Christ died for me."

We believers are part of the universal church. As in the parables of Jesus, we are only given a small glimpse of the church. It is too great for us to imagine. And yet we have been called to BE this church that we cannot see. We cannot really manage a task so great, and so once again the Holy Spirit enters in. As Jesus reached out to Peter as he began to sink into a treacherous sea, so the Spirit reaches out to us when we are floundering.

The season of Pentecost is long, about half the year. During the summer, when we are thinking about the growth of green things, when flowers are blooming, when crops are growing in the fields and on the trees, many of the Sunday texts are the parables and stories of Jesus that describe life and growth in the realm of God. During this time we meditate on our spiritual growth and health in relationship to Christ and our service towards others. We also give thanks for what has been given to us.

Toward the end of the season, we are directed to think of last things—the promises of God, the day of judgment and the resurrection of the dead. Amid the last few Sundays of Pentecost we celebrate All Saints Sunday—the remembrance of those living and dead. On that special day we remember that every member of the church is a saint.

In Madagascar, the large island off the southeast coast of the African continent, the dominant religion is the traditional indiginous religion. These people hold a great respect for their dead and honor them by offering gifts. Their dead are buried extravagantly. When the gospel was introduced, the new Malagasy saints still remembered ancestors with love but worshiped God. One of the favorite hymns of the Malagasy Church is "The Music of Heaven," which paraphrases portions of Revelation and celebrates life everlasting.

The finale of the Pentecost season is Christ the King Sunday. On this final Sunday of the Church year, we discover once again a God who is vulnerable in love for the world. Here is a king who reigns from a cross, who in a crown of thorns and a purple robe was mocked by his executioners, who abides with us today and saves us with the holy sacrifice of his own body and blood.

The liturgical color for Pentecost is red, signifying the flames and the presence of the Holy Spirit. A tongue of fire is a symbol that reminds us of the flames that descended on the heads of the disciples at Pentecost. As they spoke the word, they were understood by people of every nation gathered. The flame also reminds us of the one who is the light of the world and of our baptismal candles. Because of our baptisms, the light of Christ now shines in each of us.

A SYMBOL: A PLANT

The deeply rooted plant growing under the sun symbolizes the Church living and growing in the light of God. The season of Pentecost emphasizes life in the Spirit. We live in the community of the church, and grow in faith, hope and love with the help of the Holy Spirit.

The color for the Sundays after Pentecost is green. Green is the color of life and growth in the Spirit.

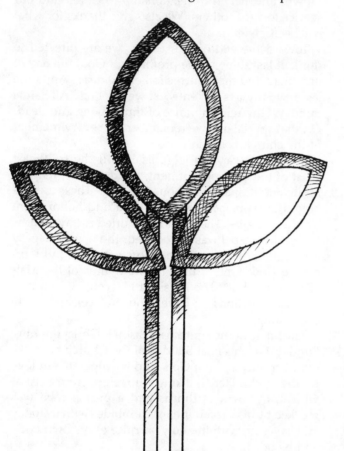

A SIGN: A FLAME

SONGS FOR PENTECOST

"Holy, Holy, Holy"
"O Day Full of Grace"
"I Love to Tell the Story"
"Amazing Grace"
"For All the Saints"
"Beautiful Savior"
"We Are One in the Spirit"
"Praise and Thanksgiving"
"I've Got the Joy"

PENTECOST ACTIVITIES

Tongues of Fire Streamers

You will need:
- bright red crepe paper
- metallic silver ribbon
- scissors

Cut 24" crepe papers and 18" ribbons. Hold an end of each together and tie in a knot. Wave the streamers in celebration in conjunction with the Pentecost story that is read during worship time.

Growing Gifts

You will need:
- plant cuttings that have roots
- clay or plastic flower pots
- potting soil
- wrapping paper prints (page 48)
- ribbon
- paper punch
- light cardboard or construction paper

Place potting soil in the flower pots and plant the cuttings. Use wrapping paper prints to wrap the pots. Lay the printed paper face down. Set the pot in the middle and tie it up around the pot with ribbon. Make prints on small cardboard or paper squares to make gift cards. Write a message on the back, such as "We are growing in the Spirit together." Punch a hole in the corner. Tie with string to the ribbon.

Give the plants to welcome Sunday morning visitors at worship.

Salt and Tempera Flames

You will need:
- salt
- dry tempera paint in red, orange, and yellow
- three bowls and spoons
- bottled glue
- paper

Mix salt with each color of tempera in a 1:1 ratio and put each in a bowl. Draw a flame with a line of glue. Put a spoon of one color of tempera on the paper and slide it over the glue. Shake the rest back into the bowl. Continue with as many flames and colors as you like as you remember the first Pentecost. Display the picture during the Pentecost season.

Celebrating Gifts

The season of Pentecost is a great time to focus on the gifts of all the members of the church. Try an intergenerational gathering around the idea of gifts. Take the opportunity in the early fall, when activities at school and in your congregation go into full swing, to celebrate the gifts of all members of your community. The service projects below highlight the gifts of all people.

Celebrate together by making the love gift (at right) or the Pentecost tree or vine (p. 47). Both crafts can be started, then dried while participants worship together. Afterward, the projects may be finished and the celebration may continue with sharing gifts of food. The love gifts may be given to those whose gifts in the community we most appreciate, such as nursing home staff members, doctors, nurses, dentists, school principals and superintendents, and the police or fire departments.

Love Gift

Life in the Spirit of the Pentecost season is life lived in love. The activity that follows reminds us of this.

You will need:
- one cube of wood, about 3" x 3" x 3", or one small gift box (jewelry size) for each person
- poster paint
- sponges cut into small (about 1") hearts, diamonds, or circles
- ribbon
- paper punch
- gold thread
- a card, about 2" x 2½", on which the following poem or something similar is printed, for each person
  Keep this gift to you from me,
  in a place where you can see.
  Remember when you're feeling blue,
  this special gift from me to you.
  This present small will always be,
  a gift of love to you from me.

Paint the block white with a sponge. Allow it to dry. Sponge paint one shape on each side of the block or the gift box with poster paint. When dry, tie a colorful ribbon around it in a bow. Make a small card that has a message of love written on it. Punch a hole in one corner; tie the card into the bow.

Pentecost Means Growing!

Pentecost is a season of growing in God's love. Make a helping hand tree or vine as a decorative banner for a church hallway or fellowship area.

You will need:
- large-sized roll paper
- brown tempera paint for the vine or the tree trunk (paint this part first)
- shallow pans (such as cake pans) with two or three layers of paper towels or napkins
- green, blue, and yellow tempera paint
- dishwashing liquid
- plastic dishpan with water, or access to a sink for cleanup
- old towels or paper towels for cleanup

Directions: Squirt paint on the paper towels in the shallow pan. Use green, blue, and yellow. Drizzle dishwashing liquid across all of the colors (this will help make cleanup easier). Invite participants to press the palms of their hands into the paint and then onto the "vine" or the "tree." The handprints will create leaves. If your group is small, more than one handprint is encouraged so that the vine or tree looks full and healthy when complete. When the banner is dry, use black marker or paint to write a message such as: "In Pentecost we grow in faith together."

World Food Day (Oct. 16)

Organize an intergenerational gathering to think about food and the global community. Invite a speaker who is acquainted with your community's needs such as someone from the local food shelf or someone from Bread for the World, ELCA World Hunger, or other agency that offers relief to a hungry world. Take an offering designated for that group.

Use the World Food Day Prayer of Thanks (based on Psalm 104) found below for devotions (p. 51).

For dinner, consider serving what a great portion of the world eats—cooked rice with a few greens. For dessert, designate 6 percent of the group as United States citizens. Inform the gathering that those living in the United States are 6 percent of the world population and get 23 percent of the food. Give this 6 percent of the group ¼ of the dessert. For example, if 50 people come to your meal and you serve 50 cookies, give three people 12 cookies and tell the other 47 people that they must divide the 38 cookies left. Or, if you serve four pans of dessert, serve an entire pan of dessert to the three and give the rest small pieces. Talk about whether it's fair, and how the situation can be made more just.

Lending a Helping Hand

Have a helping hand auction to raise money for a worthy cause. "Auction" the gifts of people in the congregation, such as washing cars, sweeping sidewalks, raking lawns, eating cookies, making conversation, and helping in a variety of ways.

International Church Birthday Party

Have an international birthday party for the church. You may play Spanish music and dance. Eat baclava from Armenia. Have a relay race by pushing a bicycle wheel rim with a broom handle, as the children do in Madagascar. Discover games and treats from other traditions from members in your own congregation.

Ask each person to bring a birthday present of pencils, pens, erasers, crayons, markers, rulers and other school items. Make Pentecost birthday gifts for children in need locally or in another part of the world. Work through a relief agency supported by your church.

Stewardship of Gifts

Use this activity to help a small group of children understand the stewardship of our gifts, especially at the time of congregational stewardship drives when adults are talking about tithing.

Get 10 pieces of candy for all but one child. Ask for a volunteer to play the part of God. Dump all the candy in front of "God." Tell the children that everything we own belongs to God, but God graciously gives it all to us. Ask "God" to give each child 10 pieces of candy. "God" should have none left. Ask if it's fair. Ask each child to give one piece back to God. Now explain that when we say we want people to tithe, we are asking that people give back a tenth of what we have to God, to whom it really belongs anyway. Ask if that is fair. Ask if it is enough. Ask how we give to God, anyway. *(By giving to our neighbors.)*

Tissue Paper Prints

During the harvest time of the year, and as Thanksgiving nears, we enjoy the gifts of the earth in a special way. Try making these prints. They can be repeated across bright tissue paper, newsprint, or other large solid colored paper to make beautiful wrapping for gifts.

You will need:
- poster paints in bright colors
- white or colored tissue paper
- fresh deciduous leaves
- scissors
- sponges
- brush
- pie tin

Prints may be made in several ways:
- Cut a sponge into the shape of an apple, heart, leaf, or another shape, dip the sponge into the paint on the pie tin and press it on a paper.
- Use cookie cutters dipped in paint and pressed on the paper.
- Brush paint on leaves or flower petals, place them face down on tissue paper and press to make prints.

Whichever method is chosen, patterns can be created by pressing the printmaking object at intervals all across the paper. Overlapping and changing colors makes for an interesting look, as does using more than one of the printmaking methods above (i.e.: heart cookie cutter and sponge hearts together).

CELEBRATING PENTECOST

A Service for the Day of Pentecost

Use the Tongues of Fire Streamers (p. 45). On a poster write this verse: "And they were all filled with the Holy Spirit and began to speak in different languages" (Acts 2:4 NRSV). You may also want to teach the "Acts 2 Rap" below to half of the group beforehand. The rest of the group should say the verse that is written on the posterboard over and over, first softly and then louder, at the same time that the rap is being said. When everyone is speaking at once, it sounds like many tongues, a reminder of the day of Pentecost.

Acts 2 Rap
Now the TWELVE were PRAYin' on PENTecost
And a GREAT wind CAME and FILLED the house
TONGUES of FIRE came DOWN on their HEADS
(wave the streamers over heads)
And they SPOKE in TONGUES as THEY were LED.

The HOly SPIRit ENtered them
and they SPOKE in DIFferent LANGuages.
And PEter told the PEOple STANDing there
THIS is what the LORD God SAYS - TO - US:
"ALL the PEOple OF these PARTS
Will reCEIVE my SPIRit IN their HEARTS
And I'll SAVE ev'ryONE who CALLS - ME - LORD.

Song: Choose a Pentecost hymn to sing. Wave the tongues of fire streamers as you sing it.

A Service Celebrating Gifts

You will need two large poster boards, rubber cement and magazine pictures of a variety of people from all walks of life. On the top of each poster board write in large block letters, "WE ARE THE CHURCH."

Leader: There are differences between us and yet each of us is wonderfully made and loved by God. God has included many different people in our family of faith. *(Invite volunteers to come forward one at a time during the litany below, and paste one of the magazine pictures on the poster. Do not worry about one-to-one correspondence with each picture. The overall effect will be of great variety.)*
Leader: As I describe the family of God, please respond, "We are the church together."
Leader: Some of us are rich.
Response: We are the church together.
Leader: Some of us are poor.
Response: We are the church together.
Leader: Some of us are young.
Response: We are the church together.
Leader: Some of us are old.
Response: We are the church together.
Leader: We are many colors.
Response: We are the church together.
Leader: We have different gifts.
Response: We are the church together.
Leader: We are different, yet we are one.
Response: We are the church together.

Scripture: 1 Corinthians 12:12-26

Leader: God made each of us different and needs us all. See the variety of people in our world? *(Draw attention to the poster.)* Together, we ARE the Church!
Prayer: God, we are all different, and yet you love us all. You made us brothers and sisters in our baptisms and gave each one of us special gifts. Help us to love one another and help one another in all that we do. Amen.

A Service Celebrating All Ages

This service may be used for an intergenerational event in the early fall. You may need the confession and litany printed for all to read.

Song: "Beautiful Savior"

PRAYER OF CONFESSION
(Based on Psalm 90)

The responses may be written out on large cards ahead of time.

Leader: O Lord, on this journey of life you have always sheltered us. Before you created the earth, or mountains or us, you were always there and you will be God forever.
All: Help us in our awareness, O God.
Leader: You see everything that we do wrong. Our life fades away like a whisper. A thousand days are like one day to you. But seventy years is all we have—eighty years, if we are strong.
All: Help us in our awareness, O God.
Leader: Teach us how short life is, so that we may use our gifts in this life wisely. Make us glad for each day that we have. Fill us each morning with your constant love, so that we may sing and be glad every day of our lives.
All: Make us glad, O God. Amen.

ASSURANCE OF PARDON
(Based on Psalm 91)

Leader: God says, "Do not be afraid. Because you have made me your refuge, I will save you and will protect you who call me Lord. When you call me, I will answer you; when you are in trouble, I will be with you. I will save you."

Scripture: 1 Samuel 3:1-10

Leader: God calls each one of us, young or old or in between, to carry the message of Jesus' love to all the world. Just as Eli and Samuel needed one another and worked together, we also ought to respect and love one another and the gifts we each bring.

With both children and adults, do this action rhyme: "Here is the church . . ." (fold hands with thumbs straight). "Here is the steeple . . ." (put pointer fingers together to make the steeple). "Open the door, see all the people . . ." (open hands and wiggle fingers). "Everyone welcome. . . ." (make wide gesture toward self). "Everyone equal. . . ." (make wide gesture outward). "Open the door, see all the people . . ." (wiggle fingers).

RESPONSIVE READING
(Based on Psalm 71)

Children: O God, I am young and I put my hope in you.
Adults: You have given me all that I have needed all my life; you have protected me since the day I was born.
Children: You teach me,
Adults: and I still tell of your wonderful acts. Now that I am old and my hair is gray, do not abandon me, O God!
Children: Let me praise you all day!
Adults: Strengthen me more and more. Be with me while I proclaim your righteousness to all the generations to come.

Song: "We Are One in the Spirit"

A Service for Trinity Sunday

Song: "Holy, Holy, Holy"
Scripture: Matthew 28:16-20

Leader: We praise you, O God, who is the mystery of Divine Three in One,
Response: With your grace and peace, now and forever.
Leader: We ask you to give us the strength of love,
Response: With your grace and peace, now and forever.
Leader: We thank you for the gift of faith,
Response: With your grace and peace, now and forever.
Leader: We trust that you offer us the promise of forgiveness,
Response: With your grace and peace, now and forever.
Leader: Be with us, your disciples, as we tell your good news,
Response: With your grace and peace, now and forever.
Leader: Be with us, your family, as we worship you together,
Response: With your grace and peace, now and forever. Amen.

On this first Sunday after Pentecost, invite those who are gathered to talk with partners about their plans for faithful growing during the season of Pentecost. This long season of "ordinary time" can be a wonderful time for meditation, journaling, and journeying with God. Mentors as well as conversational partners here might be encouraged to check in on each other's discoveries and growth at regular intervals during the season.

Song: End with a joyful hymn of praise.

A Service for World Food Day

Song: "Praise and Thanksgiving"

OFFERING
As the group sings, or silently, invite individuals to put donations of money and nonperishable foods into baskets on the altar.

PRAYER OF THANKS
(Based on Psalm 104)
Divide into three groups and read the three portions of the prayer:
Group 1: Lord, you have made so many things! How wisely you made them all! The earth is filled with your creatures. All of them depend on you to give them food when they need it. You give it to them and they eat it; you provide food and they are satisfied.
Group 2: When you turn away, they are afraid. When you take away your breath, they die and go back to the dust from which they came. But when you give them breath, they are created. You give new life to the earth.
Group 3: I will sing to the Lord all my life. As long as I live I will sing praises to my God. Praise the Lord, my soul! Praise the Lord!

See page 47 for event ideas for World Food Day.

A Service for All Saints' Day

Each participant could be given a candle. Put them in a styrofoam block with holes already made, candle holders or other secure places, and be sure there is substantial adult participation and supervision where children are participating.

Song: Choose a favorite children's song of praise.

Prayer: Dearest Jesus, we were baptized in you, and we are your saints. Help us to remember those who have lived before us in faith. Help us in our telling of the good news. You are the light of the world. Amen.

Scripture: Matthew 5:1-12, 14-16

Ask participants to respond "You are the light of the world. Help us to be lights."
Leader: At Christmas, you came to us, Jesus.
Response: You are the light of the world. Help us to be lights.
Leader: At Epiphany, starlight led the nations to you and showed everyone the miracle of your coming.
Response: You are the light of the world. Help us to be lights.
Leader: At Easter, your light overcame all the darkness of our lives—all sin, evil, and death.
Response: You are the light of the world. Help us to be lights.
Leader: In each of our baptisms, you made us the saints of God. Let our light so shine before others that they may see our good works and glorify our Father in heaven.
Response: You are the light of the world. Help us to be lights.

Silent Meditation

Participants are asked to think of saints, living or dead, and light a candle to remember them. Encourage them to pray for them or think about the way God's light has shone in their lives. Candles are lit. Candles should immediately be placed in styrofoam, candle holders, or another secure place. They can stay lighted through the final song.

Song: Sing a song about unity, such as "We Are One in the Spirit"

A Service for Christ the King Sunday

This service uses lessons and hymnody from all the seasons of the Church year, reviewing Jesus' royalty in all of its complexity with a variety of Bible texts.

Advent
Scripture: Psalm 24:7-10
Song: "Come Thou Long Expected Jesus"
Prayer: God, you once sent prophets to your people to prepare for your coming as servant and as King. Help us to tell everyone that Christ our King has come and so prepare his way; through our Lord Jesus. Amen.

Christmas
Scripture: Luke 2:8-14
Song: "Joy to the World"
Prayer: Christ the King, you made your love known in the weakness of a human child. We pray that your life will free us from sin, and give us everlasting joy. Amen.

Epiphany
Scripture: Matthew 2:1-12
Song: "Bright and Glorious Is the Sky" verses 1-3, 6
Prayer: O God, you showed the royalty of the nations Christ our King, by the leading of a star. Lead us to know your light in our lives. Amen.

Lent
Scripture: Colossians 1:13-20
Song: Choose a familiar Lenten hymn to sing.
Prayer: King of mercy, you love everything you have made and you forgive the sins of all who are sorry. Create in us new and honest hearts and let your kingdom of light break into our troubled world. Amen.

Passion Sunday
Scripture: Luke 23:35-43

Prayer: Almighty God, you sent your Son, Jesus Christ, to take our flesh upon him and to suffer death on the cross. Remember us in your kingdom and teach us to pray . . . *(All recite the Lord's Prayer).*

Easter
Scripture: John 19:38—20:18
Song: Sing a song of praise together.
Prayer: God who loves us, thank you for raising Jesus, the King of life to new life on Easter. We praise you for that new life shared with us. Amen.

Pentecost
Scripture: Jeremiah 23:2-6
Song: "The King of Love My Shepherd Is"
Prayer: O God, you sent us Jesus to be our shepherd. Help us to listen, and lead us to choose the one thing which will not be taken from us, Christ our King. Amen.

Christ the King
Scripture: Revelation 1:4b-8
Song: "Beautiful Savior"
Prayer: Almighty and everlasting God, you have given everything to your beloved Son, whom you made King of all creation. Grant that all the people of the earth may be united under the glorious and gentle rule of your Son, our Jesus Christ our King. Amen.

ABOUT CHILDREN AND CHURCH

Appreciating Where Children Fit

Jesus makes special reference to children in the Bible. He recognizes them as models of faith, open to receiving God's love and grace without condition much more easily than adults. Children are accustomed to trusting—they must depend on others to meet all of their needs. They are concerned very little with power and control; their greatest need is to be loved and cared for.

Children are part of God's family. We welcome them as members of our churches, learners and workers with people of all ages in the kingdom of God. Children offer adults a reality check as we worship and investigate our relationship with God and God's creation. Children "OOH" at the beautiful flowers and cry at the trumpets' surprise. They want to smell and touch and move to the music. They smile without fear. Children remind us how good it feels to belong first and forever to God. If we let them, they show us what AWE is all about.

While it is important that children learn about faith, it is equally important that they experience life among faithful people. For that reason alone, children need to be a part of worship. They need to see, hear, and feel firsthand what God's people do—and try it out for themselves. With help and a little flexibility, even young children can be participants in some of the reassuring rituals of worship and so grow in the faith community.

Making Worship Meaningful for Children

- Engage as many of their senses as possible.
- Provide simple worship folders with pictures of Bible stories, a few key words and ideas to explore, and the seasons' symbols in a colorable size.
- Offer "Let's Learn about Worship" times for families on Saturday morning. A minister or other worship leader introduces the space, equipment, and routines of worship as appropriate for the ages of the children.
- Encourage children and their families to sit near the front of the church so that they can see and be part of what is happening.
- Have "church bags" available for families to borrow during worship. Bags might contain quiet items such as finger puppets, picture books, small coloring books and a few crayons, and sponge or foam symbol shapes or creation figures.
- Tape record key parts of a worship service in your church (especially short responses that children will be able to learn), and send copies home with families. Suggest that they play the tapes as background for children's quiet play times, and try joining in. Such casual, comfortable encounters with worship at home can make worship at church a familiar and positive experience for people of all ages.
- Make worship meaningful for adults.

ABOUT INTERGENERATIONAL LEARNING

How Do We Learn?

Families are our first learning communities; homes are our first learning settings. We begin life dependent on the guidance and stimulation of people who are different ages from us. Peers become significant sources of learning as we grow older. But parents, grandparents, and other loving adults readily admit that children are remarkable teachers for them.

Modern society understands learning as "schooling." Even at church, we tend to value the efficiency of teaching people of particular ages and at particular skill levels together. Much of what we understand to be intergenerational learning seems chaotic, time-consuming, and just plain messy for our contemporary quantitative tastes.

But the more we study effective education for today and the future, the more we recognize the importance of lifelong interactive learning. We are pushed to continue exploring every waking minute; we are offered the joy of discovery and encouraged to embrace learning as change.

The gifts of thoughtful inquiry and committed curiosity are crucial for learners of all ages. These gifts can be effectively nurtured in the faith community by friends and family of all ages. Seeing through another's eyes and hearing through another's ears can awaken and transform. Touching, putting together, and taking apart together can change people forever.

Learning in intergenerational settings involves a commitment to cooperation and conversation. Young and old need to agree to respect one another, listen to one another, and grow with one another. Their investigations may be characterized as journeys with destinations in mind, but allowing for scheduled and unscheduled stops along the way. Learning with others is part of being created human and in relationship, central to being God's people.

Things to Remember as You Plan Intergenerational Activities

- All people, whatever their ages, abilities, and interests, are children of God.
- All people, whatever their ages, abilities, and interests, are learners and teachers.
- All people, whatever their ages, abilities, and interests, want to feel they belong and contribute.
- All people, whatever their ages, abilities, and interests, need help now and then.
- Learning is not a series of isolated experiences provided for one person by another. Learning at its best is meaningful discovery, related to past learning and pointing toward future discovery.
- Learning about faith means sharing the story, and making sure it connects with the learner's life questions. Sharing the faith throughout history has been primarily an intergenerational activity.
- Celebrate your learning as children of God.

ADVENT

ADVENT

ADVENT

What is the season of ADVENT?

Advent is the four weeks before Christmas. It is a time to slow down, wait, and prepare for the coming of God's Son Jesus into our world.

The Bible says:

Isaiah 11:1-10; Mark 1:1-8; John 1:6-8, 19-28; Luke 1:26-46

A Prayer

Be with us, God, in the darkness of December as we wait for light and wait for Jesus. Come to us with your love and peace. Amen.

To do together

Hunt for circles around your home that can remind you of the slow-down-preparation time of Advent. Decorate these unmoving wheels with bits of ribbon and strips of fabric and paper. Clocks, doorknobs, mirrors, and hanging plates (even a baseball or an almost circular tennis racquet) could be attractive and effective reminders.

Celebration Wonders

● What is the hardest thing you have had to wait for?
● What do you miss most about having fewer daylight hours?
● Why is it important to prepare for Jesus' coming?

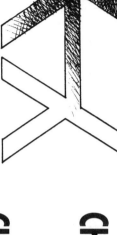

CHRISTMAS

CHRISTMAS

CHRISTMAS

What is the season of CHRISTMAS?

Christmas is a day and the 12 days that follow, during which we celebrate Jesus' birth. At Christmas the ordinary becomes extraordinary as God becomes human, a gift of love for us.

The Bible says:

Luke 2:1-20; Luke 2:41-52; Psalm 147:13-21

A Prayer

Dear God, amid the hectic pace of Christmas help us find the hallowed peace of Christmas. Thank you for Jesus, God with us, Emmanuel, our friend. Amen.

To Do Together

Jesus, who slept in a manger, was God entering our lives in the simplest, most ordinary way. Jesus meets us in the ordinary, concrete "mangers" of our daily lives. Spend a few minutes every day talking together about "mangers" where you have encountered God's gift of Jesus—a friendly smile, a found object, the red of a tree light or a sky light at sunset. Describe or draw these mangers on small pieces of paper which you can keep in a small basket near your family's crèche.

Celebration Wonders

● What makes you happiest about Christmas?
● How would you rather express the joy of Christmas: with the angels and their sky-filling songs or with the shepherds and their kneeling awe?
● What can you do to keep feeling and sharing the joy of Christmas when Christmas is over?

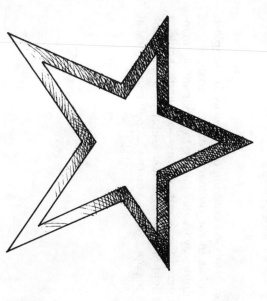

EPIPHANY

EPIPHANY

EPIPHANY

What is the season of EPIPHANY?

Epiphany is a celebration of light. As children of light, we, like the Wise Men, follow a star to meet Jesus. God is revealed as a child, and the baptized Jesus is revealed as God's beloved Son.

The Bible says:

Matthew 2:1-12; Matthew 3:13-17; Mark 1:4-11; John 2:1-11

A Prayer

Remind us, God, as we open our eyes to the light of each new day, that you are our light. Invite us to follow your light to places unknown but filled with your promise, just as wise people long ago followed your star to Jesus. Amen.

To Do Together

Read the creation stories in Genesis 1 and notice the key place that light has in the process of God's creating. Use a concordance to find and read as many references to light as you can. Record each one on a different page in a notebook or journal, and encourage all family members to use those references for personal devotions. Old and young might add thoughts, questions, and drawings to the pages in response to what they read.

Celebration Wonders

- Who has brought you the light of insight into who Jesus is?
- When and where are you especially aware of your feelings about light and darkness?
- How can one person's actions bring light to someone in need?

LENT

LENT

LENT

What is the season of LENT?

Lent is the springtime of the soul. It is a season of learning, of giving up the old ways, of anticipating newness of life.

The Bible says:

Matthew 6:1-6,16-21; Genesis 12:1-8; Luke 13:31-35; Mark 15:1-39; Luke 27:7-20; Psalm 22:1-23; John 18:1—19:42

A Prayer

Thank you, God, for the gift of your Son who died on a cross for us. Guide us and renew us as we prepare the soil of our souls to receive the springtime of your new life. Amen.

To Do Together

Find a jigsaw puzzle with a religious illustration, complicated enough to keep your family busy for some time. The number and size of pieces should be appropriate to the ages of family members. Locate a table that can have the puzzle on it for several weeks as you work on the puzzle together. The calm and patience needed for doing the puzzle may grow as part of your Lenten journey.

Celebration Wonders

● What stories have you heard about or experiences have you had with people who live Lent as a time of serious introspection and self-sacrifice?
● What parts of your life could use a thorough spring "housecleaning"?
● In what ways do you use the quiet time of winter to prepare for the challenges of life in the spring?

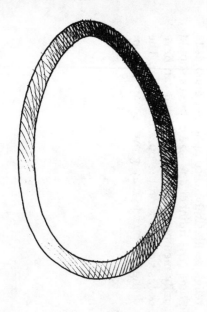

EASTER

EASTER

EASTER

What is the season of EASTER?

Easter is the highest festival of the church year. The day and the weeks that follow it celebrate Jesus' resurrection from the dead and seal God's promise of new life, an eternal YES for us.

The Bible says:

Luke 24:13-49; John 20:19-31; Acts 9:1-20

A Prayer

Hear us, God, and join in our celebration. Jesus is risen! Alleluia! Yes! He is risen indeed! Amen.

To Do Together

Every Sunday worship is, in part, a celebration of Jesus' resurrection. Explore as a family the worship book used in your church. (You may also enlist the help of your pastor or another worship leader.) Find hints or statements of that celebration in the words spoken or songs sung by members of your church family each Sunday.

Celebration Wonders

● What would your response have been to the Easter announcement of the women at the tomb?
● When has it been most difficult for you to accept life out of death?
● How might you "put on something new" to help you feel the newness of new life in Jesus?

PENTECOST

PENTECOST

PENTECOST

What is the season of PENTECOST?

Pentecost is the longest season of the church year, taking up nearly half of the year. It is a time for spiritual growth and discipleship. It is a time to study and practice the faith, guided and challenged by the Holy Spirit.

The Bible says:

Acts 2; Psalm 104; Luke 7:1-17; Luke 10:1-12; Matthew 13:1-9, 18-23; Isaiah 52:1-6; Luke 19:11-27; John 18:33-37

A Prayer

Holy Spirit, may we see you in the invisible wind and hear you in the silence of our hearts. Thank you for the gift of graceful growing. Amen.

To Do Together

Green is the color of Pentecost, and much of God's beautiful creation comes in shades of green. Make sure your family's art cupboard has a good supply of green paint, clay, paper, fabric, crayons, and markers. Have sketch pads with green chalk and green colored pencils in bags ready to go outdoors with family artists. Be on the lookout for green textures and magazine pictures of green curiosities that might stimulate family art projects.

Celebration Wonders

● When has God surprised you with something wonderful?
● Why do you think God comes to us in different ways at different times?
● Why is it exciting, challenging, and most necessary to grow in faith as long as we live?

The Magi's Journey Game

You will need:
- poster board
- black and colored markers
- buttons or other appropriate game markers
or
- masking tape or chalk
- a large floor space with a hard surface

Create a traveling game that players can use to imagine some of the difficulties and joys the Magi might have encountered on their way to see Jesus. Draw the path on poster board, with 20-25 button-sized spaces to follow. Another option is to use masking tape or chalk to create a walk-around floor game with hopscotch-like spaces along a path players will walk. The beginning of either could look like an oasis, and the end should have a biblical city skyline, lighted by a bright star.

Spaces might say (or coordinate with cards that say) things like: "You have come to an oasis. Advance 2 spaces." "The road to Herod's palace is being repaired. Take the detour and lose 1 turn." "You spilled some gold. Go back 3 spaces."

Read the story again from Matthew 2 to spark more ideas for things that could help or hinder travel progress. Possibilities include things like sandstorms, robbers, other travelers with information, Herod's men, seeing the star, good weather, and sand in your sandals.

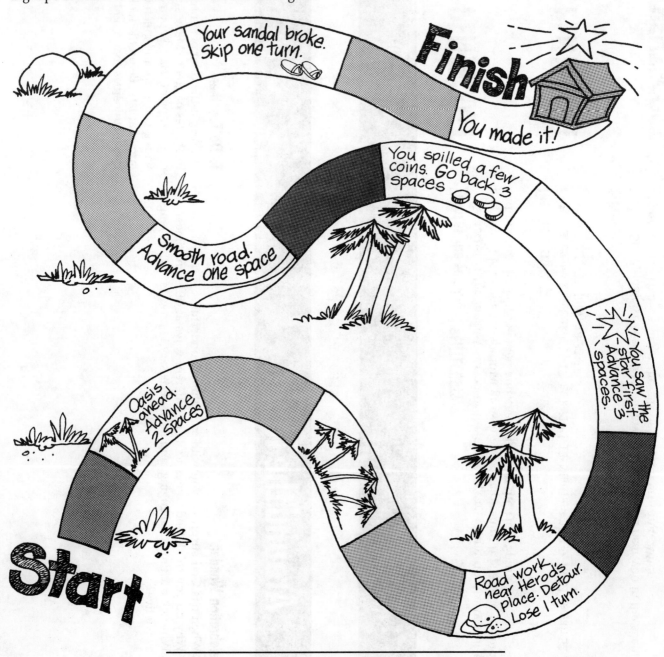

PLANNING AND REFLECTING ON THE SEASON

Season _____ Year _____

Overall goal _____

Age-level goals

_____

_____

_____

_____

_____

_____

Activities used and comments

_____

_____

_____

_____

_____

_____

Notes for next year

_____

_____

_____

_____

_____

_____

BIBLIOGRAPHY

Anderson, Sandra Myhr. *Let's Get Ready for Christmas*. Minneapolis: Augsburg, 1992.

Apostolos-Cappadona, Diane, ed. *The Sacred Play of Children*. New York: The Seabury Press, 1983.

Aschliman, Kathryn. *Growing Toward Peace*. Scottdale, PA: Herald Press, 1993.

Cavalletti, Sofia. *The Religious Potential of the Child*. New York: Paulist Press, 1983.

Erickson, Donna. *More Prime Time Together with Kids*. Minneapolis: Augsburg, 1992.

Fitzpatrick, Jean Grasso. *Something More: Nurturing Your Child's Spiritual Growth*. New York: Penguin Books, 1991.

Harris, Maria. *Fashion Me People*. Louisville: Westminster/John Knox Press, 1989.

Nelson, Gertrud Mueller. *To Dance with God*. New York: Paulist Press, 1986.

O'Neal, Debbie Trafton. *More Than Glue and Glitter: A Classroom Guide for Volunteer Teachers*. Minneapolis: Augsburg, 1992.

Ryan, G. Thomas. *Sourcebook for Sundays and Seasons*. Chicago: Liturgy Training Publications, 1994.

To Celebrate: Reshaping Holidays and Rites of Passage. Ellenwood, GA: Alternatives, 1987.